INTRODUCING
ISSUES WITH
OPPOSING
VIEWPOINTS®

Violence

Jacqueline Langwith, *Book Editor*

GREENHAVEN PRESS
A part of Gale, Cengage Learning

GALE
CENGAGE Learning™

Detroit • New York • San Francisco • New Haven, Conn • Waterville, Maine • London

Christine Nasso, *Publisher*
Elizabeth Des Chenes, *Managing Editor*

© 2010 Greenhaven Press, a part of Gale, Cengage Learning

LIBRARY OF CONGRESS CATALOGING-IN-PUBLICATION DATA

Violence / Jacqueline Langwith, book editor.
    p. cm. -- (Introducing issues with opposing viewpoints)
  Includes bibliographical references and index.
  ISBN 978-0-7377-4736-2 (hardcover)
  1. Violence--Juvenile literature. 2. Violence--Prevention--Juvenile literature.
  I. Langwith, Jacqueline.
  HM886.V53 2010
  303.6--dc22

                                                                    2009050039

Printed in the United States of America
1 2 3 4 5 6 7 14 13 12 11 10

Contents

Foreword

I ndulging in a wide spectrum of ideas, beliefs, and perspectives is a critical cornerstone of democracy. After all, it is often debates over differences of opinion, such as whether to legalize abortion, how to treat prisoners, or when to enact the death penalty, that shape our society and drive it forward. Such diversity of thought is frequently regarded as the hallmark of a healthy and civilized culture. As the Reverend Clifford Schutjer of the First Congregational Church in Mansfield, Ohio, declared in a 2001 sermon, "Surrounding oneself with only like-minded people, restricting what we listen to or read only to what we find agreeable is irresponsible. Refusing to entertain doubts once we make up our minds is a subtle but deadly form of arrogance." With this advice in mind, Introducing Issues with Opposing Viewpoints books aim to open readers' minds to the critically divergent views that comprise our world's most important debates.

Introducing Issues with Opposing Viewpoints simplifies for students the enormous and often overwhelming mass of material now available via print and electronic media. Collected in every volume is an array of opinions that captures the essence of a particular controversy or topic. Introducing Issues with Opposing Viewpoints books embody the spirit of nineteenth-century journalist Charles A. Dana's axiom: "Fight for your opinions, but do not believe that they contain the whole truth, or the only truth." Absorbing such contrasting opinions teaches students to analyze the strength of an argument and compare it to its opposition. From this process readers can inform and strengthen their own opinions, or be exposed to new information that will change their minds. Introducing Issues with Opposing Viewpoints is a mosaic of different voices. The authors are statesmen, pundits, academics, journalists, corporations, and ordinary people who have felt compelled to share their experiences and ideas in a public forum. Their words have been collected from newspapers, journals, books, speeches, interviews, and the Internet, the fastest growing body of opinionated material in the world.

Introducing Issues with Opposing Viewpoints shares many of the well-known features of its critically acclaimed parent series, Opposing Viewpoints. The articles are presented in a pro/con format, allowing readers to absorb divergent perspectives side by side. Active reading questions preface each viewpoint, requiring the student to approach the material thoughtfully and carefully. Useful charts, graphs, and cartoons supplement each article. A thorough introduction provides readers with crucial background on an issue. An annotated bibliography points the reader toward articles, books, and Web sites that contain additional information on the topic. An appendix of organizations to contact contains a wide variety of charities, nonprofit organizations, political groups, and private enterprises that each hold a position on the issue at hand. Finally, a comprehensive index allows readers to locate content quickly and efficiently.

Introducing Issues with Opposing Viewpoints is also significantly different from Opposing Viewpoints. As the series title implies, its presentation will help introduce students to the concept of opposing viewpoints and learn to use this material to aid in critical writing and debate. The series' four-color, accessible format makes the books attractive and inviting to readers of all levels. In addition, each viewpoint has been carefully edited to maximize a reader's understanding of the content. Short but thorough viewpoints capture the essence of an argument. A substantial, thought-provoking essay question placed at the end of each viewpoint asks the student to further investigate the issues raised in the viewpoint, compare and contrast two authors' arguments, or consider how one might go about forming an opinion on the topic at hand. Each viewpoint contains sidebars that include at-a-glance information and handy statistics. A Facts About section located in the back of the book further supplies students with relevant facts and figures.

Following in the tradition of the Opposing Viewpoints series, Greenhaven Press continues to provide readers with invaluable exposure to the controversial issues that shape our world. As John Stuart Mill once wrote: "The only way in which a human being can make some approach to knowing the whole of a subject is by hearing what can be said about it by persons of every variety of opinion and studying all modes in which it can be looked at by every character of mind. No wise man ever acquired his wisdom in any mode but this." It is to this principle that Introducing Issues with Opposing Viewpoints books are dedicated.

Introduction

"Bullying should not be considered a normal part of childhood or adolescence, but rather as a marker for more serious violent behaviors."

—Elizabeth M. Duke, U.S. Health Resources
and Services Administration

An article in the July 9, 2009, *Miami Herald* tells the story of eleven-year-old Carl Walker-Hoover. In April 2009 Carl's mother, Sirdeaner, found him hanging from the ceiling with an extension cord around his neck. Sirdeaner was devastated and wanted to know what could make her young son so distraught that he would take his own life. She soon found that Carl had been the victim of bullying. According to Sirdeaner, "All year, bullies had been making his life miserable, calling him a 'faggot' and threatening to kill him." Stories like Carl's are common all around the country. The U.S. Centers for Disease Control and Prevention estimates that each year nearly one-third of sixth to tenth graders in the United States are involved in bullying, either as victims or as perpetrators.

Bullying is doing or saying something to another person to intimidate him or her. Power is a very important factor in bullying. Bullies try to intimidate their victims in order to gain power over them. Bullying can take many forms, including name calling, teasing, saying or writing nasty things, leaving people out of activities, ignoring them, threatening them, scaring them, making them feel uncomfortable, taking or damaging their belongings, hitting or kicking them, or making them do things they do not want to do. Verbal bullying is the most common type of bullying inflicted on both boys and girls. However, boys are more likely to be physically bullied, while girls who are bullied are more likely to be the subject of false rumors, receive sexual comments, or be socially excluded.

Certain young people seem to be the target of bullying. Kids who are different in some way are often bullied. For example, kids may be bullied because of their race or ethnicity, because they talk differently, because of their social class, because they are quiet or shy, because they are small or large, or for many different reasons. Bullying can be unbearable for some children. It can make young people feel insecure, lonely, unhappy, and frightened. Many kids who are bullied get physically sick and miss a lot of school. In her essay "Beyond Bullying" on the Web site Wiretap.org, Latricia Wilson wrote about the devastation she felt after she moved from Indiana to Tennessee and was befriended by a girl who eventually became her bully:

> I became more isolated and depressed. I lost weight and found myself crying hysterically at times, unable to calm down after being humiliated at school. In my mind, my childhood bully seemed to have turned the whole world against me. I hated her for that and I hated myself for the emotional abuse I endured, which I believed I had caused. There were times I contemplated suicide and times I wished my bully would die. On many occasions I took Benadryl and sleeping pills just to get some peace and rest. I saw a psychologist from time to time and was prescribed various anti-depressive medications. Eventually, I suffered a nervous breakdown and had to be taken out of school.

Latricia's suicidal feelings are common for kids who are the victims of bullying. Indeed, the outcome of bullying can be deadly. Some children, like Carl Walker-Hoover, not only think about suicide but carry through with it. Bullying may also contribute to the mind-set that creates school shooters. Paducah, Kentucky, school shooter Michael Carneal and Columbine killers Eric Harris and Dylan Klebold were victims of bullying.

Kids bully other kids for many reasons. Some kids see bullying as a way of being popular or making themselves look tough and "cool." Some bully to get attention or to make other people afraid of them. Sometimes bullies are jealous of the kids they torment. Other times they themselves may even be victims of bullying. Michael Brumfield is a stay-at-home dad from Ohio, who in an article on Hubpages.com admits to being a bully when he was younger. Brumfield discusses why he bullied:

I didn't bully those who were weaker than me. I bullied the people who thought that they were better than me. The poor kids thought that they were tougher, the preps thought that they were richer, the geeks thought that they were smarter, and the jocks thought that they were stronger. I had something to prove to them and myself. I wanted to show them all that I saw and exploit their "weakness." I wish that I would have seen this while I was still in school and stop[ped] myself from doing it.

A young woman from Canada submitted the following comment on the Web site Bullying.org about why she was a bully:

I remember all my life picking on people, mostly other girls that I thought were funny looking, or girls that didn't have designer clothes. I used to pretend to be nice to them, spread rumors about them while I was pretending to be their friend. I used to flirt with guys that were considered as nerds, and then try to get them beat up. I was a really big b****, and I realize now that it isn't right to do that, everyone is equal. I think I just did it to make people laugh at me, to make me feel good about myself, because I had really low self-esteem.

Researchers have tried to understand more about why some kids are bullies. A study by researchers at York and Queens Universities in Canada, which was published in 2008, found that children who bullied "tended to be aggressive and lacking in a moral compass and they experienced a lot of conflict in their relationships with their parents. In addition, their relationships with friends also were marked by a lot of conflict, and they tended to associate with others who bullied." The American Psychological Association (APA) says that children are more likely to bully if warmth and parent involvement are lacking in their lives or if they receive harsh corporal punishment. Bullying is an early form of aggressive, violent behavior. According to the APA, an estimated one in four boys who bully will have a criminal record by age thirty.

The U.S. Substance Abuse and Mental Health Services Administration (SAMHSA) says parents and other adults are the key to stopping bullying. Bullies need positive role models and adults to teach them that violence and bullying are not acceptable. Children who are victims of bullying need to seek help from parents or other caring adults. According to SAMHSA, when adults and other kids fail to recognize and stop bullying behavior as it occurs, they are actually promoting violence. They are saying to the bully, "You have the right to hurt people," and to the victim, "You are not worth protecting."

Bullying is a form of violence that many young people deal with on a daily basis. Unfortunately, it is just one of many forms of violence in the world today. In *Introducing Issues with Opposing Viewpoints: Violence,* many people offer their opinions on the causes of violence, its role in the world, and how to prevent it.

Chapter 1

What Causes Violence?

The roots of violence are the subject of much debate, with researchers reporting various causes for violent behavior, including societal factors, religion, violence in the media, brain circuitry, and genetics.

Religion Causes Violence

Christopher Hitchens

"**Religion poisons everything.** *As well as a menace to civilization, it has become a threat to human survival.*"

In the following viewpoint Christopher Hitchens contends that religion causes violence, destruction, and death. In response to a hypothetical question issued by a religious commentator, Hitchens describes how religion has caused massacres and death in six cities—Belfast, Beirut, Bombay, Belgrade, Bethlehem, and Baghdad. Hitchens also says that the 9/11 terrorists were motivated by religious beliefs. According to Hitchens, religion kills. Hitchens is an author, journalist, political observer, and literary critic. This excerpt is from his book *God Is Not Great: How Religion Poisons Everything.*

AS YOU READ, CONSIDER THE FOLLOWING QUESTIONS:
1. According to Hitchens, religion must seek to interfere with the lives of nonbelievers because it wants what?
2. According to Hitchens, what city used to be called the Paris of the Orient?
3. According to Hitchens, anyone concerned with human safety or dignity would have to hope for a mass outbreak of what?

I magine that you can perform a feat of which I am incapable. Imagine, in other words, that you can picture an infinitely benign and all-powerful creator, who conceived of you, then made and shaped you, brought you into the world he had made for you, and now supervises and cares for you even while you sleep. Imagine, further, that if you obey the rules and commandments that he has lovingly prescribed, you will qualify for an eternity of bliss and repose. I do not say that I envy you this belief (because to me it seems like the wish for a horrible form of benevolent and unalterable dictatorship), but I do have a sincere question. Why does such a belief not make its adherents happy? It must seem to them that they have come into possession of a marvelous secret, of the sort that they could cling to in moments of even the most extreme adversity.

It Is About Power

Superficially, it does sometimes seem as if this is the case. I have been to evangelical services, in black and in white communities, where the whole event was one long whoop of exaltation at being saved, loved, and so forth. Many services, in all denominations and among almost all pagans, are exactly designed to evoke celebration and communal fiesta, which is precisely why I suspect them. There are more restrained and sober and elegant moments, also. When I was a member of the Greek Orthodox Church, I could feel, even if I could not believe, the joyous words that are exchanged between believers on Easter morning: "*Christos anesti!*" (Christ is risen!) "*Alethos anest!*" (He is risen indeed!) I was a member of the Greek Orthodox Church, I might add, for a reason that explains why very many people profess an outward allegiance. I joined it to please my Greek parents-in-law. The archbishop who received me into his communion on the same day that he officiated at my wedding, thereby trousering two fees instead of the usual one, later became an enthusiastic cheerleader and fund-raiser for his fellow Orthodox Serbian mass murderers Radovan Karadzic and Ratko Mladic, who filled countless mass graves all over Bosnia. The next time I got married, which was by a Reform Jewish rabbi with an Einsteinian and Shakespearean bent, I had something a little more in common with the officiating person. But even he was aware that his lifelong homosexuality was, in principle, condemned as a capital offense, punishable by the founders of his religion by stoning. As to the

Anglican Church into which I was originally baptized, it may look like a pathetic bleating sheep today, but as the descendant of a church that has always enjoyed a state subsidy and an intimate relationship with hereditary monarchy, it has a historic responsibility for the Crusades, for persecution of Catholics, Jews, and Dissenters, and for combat against science and reason.

The level of intensity fluctuates according to time and place, but it can be stated as a truth that religion does not, and in the long run cannot, be content with its own marvelous claims and sublime assurances. It *must* seek to interfere with the lives of nonbelievers, or heretics, or adherents of other faiths. It may speak about the bliss of the next world, but it wants power in this one. This is only to be expected. It is, after all, wholly man-made. And it does not have the confidence in its own various preachings even to allow coexistence between different faiths. . . .

The Question

A week before the events of September 11, 2001, I was on a panel with Dennis Prager, who is one of America's better-known religious broadcasters. He challenged me in public to answer what he called a "straight yes/no question," and I happily agreed. Very well, he said. I was to imagine myself in a strange city as the evening was coming on. Toward me I was to imagine that I saw a large group of men approaching. Now—would I feel safer, or less safe, if I was to learn that they were just coming from a prayer meeting? As the reader will see, this is not a question to which a yes/no answer can be given. But I was able to answer it as if it were not hypothetical. "Just to stay within the letter 'B,' I have actually had that experience in Belfast, Beirut, Bombay, Belgrade, Bethlehem, and Baghdad. In each case I can say absolutely, and can give my reasons, why I would feel immediately threatened if I thought that the group of men approaching me in the dusk were coming from a religious observance."

Belfast

Here, then, is a very brief summary of the religiously inspired cruelty I witnessed in these six places. In Belfast, I have seen whole streets burned out by sectarian warfare between different sects of Christianity, and interviewed people whose relatives and friends have

Religious Conflicts and Attacks

Kosovo (Serbia)
LEBANON
Arctic Ocean
Moscow
BRITAIN
Chechnya (Russia)
Xinjang (China)
New York
SPAIN
IRAQ
AFGHANISTAN
Washington
MOROCCO
Kashmir (India/Pakistan)
ALGERIA
PAKISTAN
MEXICO
EGYPT
SAUDI
INDIA
THAILAND
SUDAN
ARABIA
PHILIPPINES
GUATEMALA
NIGERIA
ETHIOPIA
SRI
Sulawesi
KENYA
LANKA
(Indonesia)
Atlantic Ocean
ISRAEL/
Bali (Indonesia)
Pacific Ocean
PALESTINE
SOMALIA
Indian Ocean

✳ Interdenominational conflict
✳ Religion-linked terrorist attacks

Taken from: *Economist*, "New Wars of Religion," November 1, 2007.

been kidnapped and killed or tortured by rival religious death squads, often for no other reason than membership of another confession. There is an old Belfast joke about the man stopped at a roadblock and asked his religion. When he replies that he is an atheist he is asked, "Protestant or Catholic atheist?" I think this shows how the obsession has rotted even the legendary local sense of humor. In any case, this did actually happen to a friend of mine and the experience was decidedly not an amusing one. . . .

Beirut

When I first saw Beirut, in the summer of 1975, it was still recognizable as "the Paris of the Orient." Yet this apparent Eden was infested with a wide selection of serpents. It suffered from a positive surplus of religions, all of them "accommodated" by a sectarian state constitution. The president by law had to be a Christian, usually a Maronite Catholic, the speaker of the parliament a Muslim, and so on. This never worked well, because it institutionalized differences of belief as well as of caste and ethnicity (the Shia Muslims were at the bottom of the social scale, the Kurds were disenfranchised altogether).

The main Christian party was actually a Catholic militia called the Phalange, or "Phalanx," and had been founded by a Maronite Lebanese named Pierre Gemayel who had been very impressed by his visit to Hitler's Berlin Olympics in 1936. It was later to achieve international notoriety by conducting the massacre of Palestinians at the Sabra and Chatila refugee camps in 1982, while acting under the orders of [Israeli] General Ariel Sharon. That a Jewish general should collaborate with a fascist party may seem grotesque enough, but they had a common Muslim enemy and that was enough. Israel's irruption into Lebanon that year also gave an impetus to the birth of Hezbollah, the modestly named "Party of God," which mobilized the Shia underclass and gradually placed it under the leadership of the theocratic dictatorship in Iran that had come to power three years previously. It was in lovely Lebanon, too, having learned to share the kidnapping business with the ranks of organized crime, that the faithful moved on to introduce us to the beauties of suicide bombing. I can still see that severed head in the road outside the near-shattered French embassy. On the whole, I tended to cross the street when the prayer meetings broke up.

> **FAST FACT**
>
> In 2007 approximately fourteen thousand terrorist incidents occurred worldwide, causing twenty-two thousand deaths, according to the National Counterterrorism Center.

Bombay

Bombay also used to be considered a pearl of the Orient, with its necklace of lights along the corniche and its magnificent British Raj architecture. It was one of India's most diverse and plural cities, and its many layers of texture have been cleverly explored by [novelist] Salman Rushdie—especially in *The Moor's Last Sigh*—and in the films of Mira Nair. It is true that there had been intercommunal fighting there, during the time in 1947–48 when the grand historic movement for Indian self-government was being ruined by Muslim demands for a separate state and by the fact that the Congress Party was led by a pious Hindu. But probably as many people took refuge in Bombay during that moment of religious bloodlust as were driven or fled from it. A form of cultural coexistence resumed, as often happens when cities are exposed to the sea and to influences from outside. Parsis—former Zoroastrians who had been persecuted in Persia—were a prominent minority, and the city was also host to a historically significant community of Jews. But this was not enough to content Mr. Bal Thackeray and his Shiv Sena Hindu nationalist movement, who in the 1990s decided that Bombay should be run by and for his coreligionists, and who loosed a tide of goons and thugs onto the streets. Just to show he could do it, he ordered the city renamed as "Mumbai," which is partly why I include it in this list under its traditional title.

Belgrade

Belgrade had until the 1980s been the capital of Yugoslavia, or the land of the southern Slavs, which meant by definition that it was the capital of a multiethnic and multiconfessional state. But a secular Croatian intellectual once gave me a warning that, as in Belfast, took the form of a sour joke. "If I tell people that I am an atheist and a Croat," he said, "people ask me how I can prove I am not a Serb." To be Croatian, in other words, is to be Roman Catholic. To be a Serb is to be Christian Orthodox. In the 1940s, this meant a Nazi puppet state, set up in Croatia and enjoying the patronage of the Vatican, which naturally sought to exterminate all the Jews in the region but also undertook a campaign of forcible conversion directed at the other Christian community. Tens of thousands of Orthodox Christians were either slaughtered or deported in consequence, and a vast concentration camp was set up near the town of Jasenovacs. So disgusting was the regime of General Ante Pavelic and his Ustashe party that even many German officers protested at having to be associated with it.

By the time I visited the site of the Jasenovacs camp in 1992, the jackboot was somewhat on the other foot. The Croatian cities of Vukovar and Dubrovnik had been brutally shelled by the armed forces of Serbia, now under the control of Slobodan Milosevic. The mainly Muslim city of Sarajevo had been encircled and was being bombarded around the clock. Elsewhere in Bosnia-Herzegovina, especially along

In 1992 the Yugoslavian city of Sarajevo was repeatedly shelled by Serbian forces in an effort to "ethnically cleanse" Sarajevo of Muslims.

the river Drina, whole towns were pillaged and massacred in what the Serbs themselves termed "ethnic cleansing." In point of fact, "religious cleansing" would have been nearer the mark. . . .

Bethlehem

As for Bethlehem, I suppose I would be willing to concede to Mr. Prager that on a good day, I would feel safe enough standing around outside the Church of the Nativity as evening came on. It is in Bethlehem, not far from Jerusalem, that many believe that, with the cooperation of an immaculately conceived virgin, god was delivered of a son.

"Now the birth of Jesus Christ was in this wise. When his mother, Mary, was espoused to Joseph, before they came together she was found with child of the Holy Ghost." Yes, and the Greek demigod Perseus was born when the god Jupiter visited the virgin Danaë as a shower of gold and got her with child. The god Buddha was born through an opening in his mother's flank. Catlicus the serpent-skirted caught a little ball of feathers from the sky and hid it in her bosom, and the Aztec god Huitzilopochtli was thus conceived. The virgin Nana took a pomegranate from the tree watered by the blood of the slain Agdestris, and laid it in her bosom, and gave birth to the god Atris. The virgin daughter of a Mongol king awoke one night and found herself bathed in a great light, which caused her to give birth to Genghis Khan. Krishna was born of the virgin Devaka. Horus was born of the virgin Isis. Mercury was born of the virgin Maia. Romulus was born of the virgin Rhea Sylvia. For some reason, many religions force themselves to think of the birth canal as a one-way street, and even the Koran treats the Virgin Mary with reverence. However, this made no difference during the Crusades, when a papal army set out to recapture Bethlehem and Jerusalem from the Muslims, incidentally destroying many Jewish communities and sacking heretical Christian Byzantium along the way, and inflicted a massacre in the narrow streets of Jerusalem, where, according to the hysterical and gleeful chroniclers, the spilled blood reached up to the bridles of the horses. . . .

I once heard the late Abba Eban, one of Israel's more polished and thoughtful diplomats and statesmen, give a talk in New York. The first thing to strike the eye about the Israeli-Palestinian dispute, he said, was the ease of its solubility. From this arresting start he went on to say, with the authority of a former foreign minister and UN representative, that the essential point was a simple one. Two peoples of roughly equivalent size had a claim to the same land. The solution was, obviously, to create two states side by side. Surely something so self-evident was within the wit of man to encompass? And so it would have been, decades ago, if the messianic rabbis and mullahs and priests could have been kept out of it. But the exclusive claims to god-given authority, made by hysterical clerics on both sides and further stoked by Armageddon-minded Christians who hope to bring on the Apocalypse (preceded by the death or conversion of all Jews), have made the situation insufferable, and put the whole of humanity in the position of hostage to a quarrel that now features the threat of nuclear war. *Religion poisons everything.* As well as a menace to civilization, it has become a threat to human survival.

Baghdad

To come last to Baghdad. This is one of the greatest centers of learning and culture in history. It was here that some of the lost works of

Aristotle and other Greeks ("lost" because the Christian authorities had burned some, suppressed others, and closed the schools of philosophy, on the grounds that there could have been no useful reflections on morality before the preaching of Jesus) were preserved, retranslated, and transmitted via Andalusia back to the ignorant "Christian" West. Baghdad's libraries and poets and architects were renowned. Many of these attainments took place under Muslim caliphs, who sometimes permitted and as often repressed their expression, but Baghdad also bears the traces of ancient Chaldean and Nestorian Christianity, and was one of the many centers of the Jewish diaspora. Until the late 1940s, it was home to as many Jews as were living in Jerusalem.

I am not here going to elaborate a position on the overthrow of Saddam Hussein in April 2003. I shall simply say that those who regarded his regime as a "secular" one are deluding themselves. . . . Saddam had inscribed the words *"Allahu akbar"*—"God Is Great"— on the Iraqi flag. He had sponsored a huge international conference of holy warriors and mullahs, and maintained very warm relations with their other chief state sponsor in the region, namely the genocidal government of Sudan. He had built the largest mosque in the region, and named it the "Mother of All Battles" mosque, complete with a Koran written in blood that he claimed to be his own. When launching his own genocidal campaign against the (mainly Sunni) people of Kurdistan—a campaign that involved the thoroughgoing use of chemical atrocity weapons and the murder and deportation of hundreds of thousands of people—he had called it "Operation *Anfal*," borrowing by this term a Koranic justification— "The Spoils" of sura 8—for the despoilment and destruction of nonbelievers. . . .

At a minimum, it can be agreed by all that the Iraqi people had endured much in the preceding thirty-five years of war and dictatorship, that the Saddam regime could not have gone on forever as an outlaw system within international law, and therefore that—whatever objections there might be to the actual means of "regime change"—the whole society deserved a breathing space in which to consider reconstruction and reconciliation. Not one single minute of breathing space was allowed.

Everybody knows the sequel. The supporters of al-Qaeda, led by a Jordanian jailbird named Abu Musab al-Zarqawi, launched a frenzied campaign of murder and sabotage. They not only slew unveiled women and secular journalists and teachers. They not only set off bombs in Christian churches (Iraq's population is perhaps 2 percent Christian) and shot or maimed Christians who made and sold alcohol. They not only made a video of the mass shooting and throat-cutting of a contingent of Nepalese guest workers, who were assumed to be Hindu and thus beyond all consideration. These atrocities might be counted as more or less routine. They directed the most toxic part of their campaign of terror at fellow Muslims. The mosques and funeral processions of the long-oppressed Shiite majority were blown up. Pilgrims coming long distances to the newly accessible shrines at Karbala and Najaf did so at the risk of their lives. In a letter to his leader Osama bin Laden, Zarqawi gave the two main reasons for this extraordinarily evil policy. In the first place, as he wrote, the Shiites were heretics who did not take the correct Salafist path of purity. They were thus a fit prey for the truly holy. In the second place, if a religious war could be induced within Iraqi society, the plans of the "crusader" West could be set at naught. . . .

An Answer

In all the cases I have mentioned, there were those who protested in the name of religion and who tried to stand athwart the rising tide of fanaticism and the cult of death. I can think of a handful of priests and bishops and rabbis and imams who have put humanity ahead of their own sect or creed. History gives us many other such examples. . . . This is a compliment to humanism, not to religion. . . . But the general reluctance of clerical authorities to issue unambiguous condemnation, whether it is the Vatican in the case of Croatia or the Saudi or Iranian leaderships in the case of their respective confessions, is uniformly disgusting. And so is the willingness of each "flock" to revert to atavistic [ancestral] behavior under the least provocation.

No, Mr. Prager, I have not found it a prudent rule to seek help as the prayer meeting breaks up. And this, as I told you, is only the letter "B." In all these cases, anyone concerned with human safety or dignity would have to hope fervently for a mass outbreak of democratic and republican secularism. . . .

9/11 Makes Answer Clear

Everybody has their own 9/11 story: I shall skip over mine except to say that someone I slightly knew was flown into the wall of the Pentagon having managed to call her husband and give a description of her murderers and their tactics (and having learned from him that it was not a hijack and that she was going to die). From the roof of my building in Washington, I could see the smoke rising from the other side of the river, and I have never since passed the Capitol or the White House without thinking of what might have happened were it not for the courage and resourcefulness of the passengers on the fourth plane, who managed to bring it down in a Pennsylvanian field only twenty minutes' flying time from its destination.

Well, I was able to write in a further reply to Dennis Prager, now you have your answer. The nineteen suicide murderers of New York and Washington and Pennsylvania were beyond any doubt the most sincere believers on those planes. Perhaps we can hear a little less about how "people of faith" possess moral advantages that others can only envy. And what is to be learned from the jubilation and the ecstatic propaganda with which this great feat of fidelity has been greeted in the Islamic world? At the time, the United States had an attorney general named John Ashcroft, who had stated that America had "no king but Jesus" (a claim that was exactly two words too long). It had a president who wanted to hand over the care of the poor to "faith-based" institutions. Might this not be a moment where the light of reason, and the defense of a society that separated church and state and valued free expression and free inquiry, be granted a point or two?

EVALUATING THE AUTHOR'S ARGUMENTS:

In this viewpoint Christopher Hitchens describes what he says is religion-caused violence and destruction in six different cities. Do you think the cities he chose provide good examples of religion-associated violence? Do you think there could be other causes for the violence Hitchens describes in these cities? Explain your answer.

Religion Does Not Cause Violence

"One can easily show that the majority of Christians— and the majority of religious folks in general— are nonviolent citizens, peace lovers, peacemakers and peace activists, not in spite of their religion but out of religious reasons."

Miroslav Volf

In the following viewpoint, Miroslav Volf argues that although misconceptions about the violent character of Christianity thrive, the majority of Christians are peaceful because of their religion. Volf contends that violence is not caused by religion, but instead by the misconceptions of the Christian faith that lead to misbehavior of Christians. Miroslav Volf is a professor at Yale Divinity School.

Miroslav Volf, "Guns and Crosses. (Faith Matters)," *Christian Century*, May 17, 2003. Reproduced by permission.

Many intellectuals associate religion—and Christianity in particular—with violence. Hence they argue that the less religion we have the better off we will be. In an article in the *Atlantic,* for example, Jonathan Rauch argues that the greatest development in modern religion is "apatheism"—a sense of not caring one way or the other whether God exists. The best of all possible situations, says Rauch, is to be indifferent toward religion, whether you are religious or not.

Misconceptions of Faith

On the pages of this journal and elsewhere, I have argued the opposite. If we strip Christian convictions of their original and historic cognitive and moral content, and reduce faith to a cultural resource endowed with a diffuse aura of the sacred, we are likely to get religiously legitimized and inspired violence in situations of conflict. If, on the other hand, we nurture people in historic Christian convictions that are rooted in sacred texts, we will likely get militants for peace. This is a result of a careful examination of two things: the inner logic of Christian convictions and actual Christian practice. In his book *The Ambivalence of the Sacred,* R. Scott Appleby argues that on the basis of case studies, and contrary to widespread misconception, religious people play a positive role in the world of human conflicts and contribute to peace—not when they "moderate their religion or marginalize their deeply held, vividly symbolized and often highly particular beliefs," but rather "when they remain religious actors."

Even if this argument is sound (as I think it is), we still need to ask why misconceptions about the violent character of Christian faith abound. I have already given part of the answer: Christians have used and continue to use their faith to legitimize violence when they believe violence must be deployed. Misconceptions of the Christian faith mirror widespread misbehavior of Christians, and misbehavior of Christians goes hand in hand with misconstruing their own faith, and with "thinning" its original elements.

There is more. One can easily show that the majority of Christians—and the majority of religious folks in general—are nonviolent citizens, peace lovers, peacemakers and peace activists, not in spite of their religion but out of religious reasons. The purveyors of violence who seek religious legitimation are statistically a small minority among Christians.

So why is the contrary opinion widespread? What Avishai Margalit writes about ethnic belonging applies equally well to religion. "It takes one cockroach found in your food to turn the otherwise delicious meal into a bad experience. . . . It takes 30 to 40 ethnic groups who are fighting one another to make the 1,500 or more significant ethnic groups in the world who live more or less peacefully look bad." One may describe this as "self-inflation of the negative," or the tendency of the evil to loom larger than the comparatively much larger good.

This tendency is strengthened in the modern world, where information flow is dominated by mass media. Consider the following contrast. The Serbian paramilitary who rapes Muslim women

FAST FACT

The Catholic Church is estimated to be the largest religious group in the world with 1.1 billion members, followed by Sunni Islam with 875 million members.

with a cross around his neck has made it into the headlines and is immortalized in books on religious violence. But Katarina Kruhonja, a medical doctor from Osijek, Croatia, and a recipient of the alternative Nobel Prize for her peace initiatives, remains relatively unknown, as does the motivation for her work, which is thoroughly religious. While it's true that the success of such work depends on low visibility, our unawareness of it also has to do with the character of mass-media communication in a market-driven world. Violence sells, so viewers get to see violence.

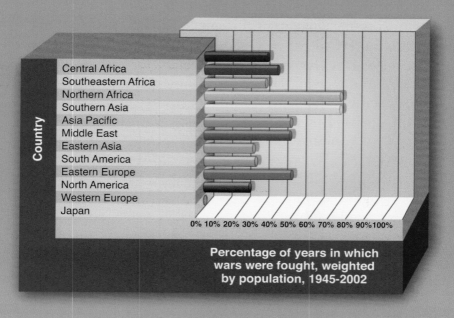

Proportion of Time Spent at War

Central Africa
Southeastern Africa
Northern Africa
Southern Asia
Asia Pacific
Middle East
Eastern Asia
South America
Eastern Europe
North America
Western Europe
Japan

Country

0% 10% 20% 30% 40% 50% 60% 70% 80% 90% 100%

Percentage of years in which wars were fought, weighted by population, 1945-2002

Taken from: Worldmapper.org. SASI Group (University of Sheffield) and Mark Newman (University of Michigan).

Why Religion?

The mass media create reality, but they do so by building on the proclivities of viewers. Why does the Serbian paramilitary rapist seem more "interesting" than Kruhonja? And why are we prone to conclude that his religious faith is implicated in the acts because he is wearing a cross, while it would never occur to us to blame the institution of marriage when we see a ring on his finger? Religion is more associated with violence than with peace in the public imagination partly because the public is fascinated with violence. We, the peace-loving citizens of nations whose tranquillity is secured by effective policing, are insatiable observers of violence. And as voyeurs, we become vicarious participants in the very violence we outwardly abhor. We are particularly drawn to religious violence because we have a strong interest in exposing hypocrisy, especially of a religious kind. Put the two factors together—the inner deployment of violence and the delight in exposure—and it looks as if we want to hear about religious people's engagement in violence because we are violent, but expect them to act otherwise.

If we were more self-critical about our violent proclivities and more suspicious about violence in media, we might note, on the religious landscape, the steady flow of work that religious people do to make the world a more peaceful place. Our imagination would not be captured, for instance, with religion as motivating force for a dozen or so not particularly religious terrorists who destroyed the Twin Towers. Instead, we would be impressed with the degree to which religion serves as a source of solace and orientation for a majority of Americans in a time of crisis. We'd note the motivation it gave to many to help the victims, protect Muslims from stereotyping, and build bridges between religious cultures. We should promote religion—this kind of religion—and not be indifferent toward it.

EVALUATING THE AUTHORS' ARGUMENTS:

In this viewpoint Miroslav Volf's fundamental argument is that the media focus on the small minority of people seeking religious legitimization for their violent acts, which continues to spread the misconception that Christianity causes violence. Contrast Volf's argument with that of Christopher Hitchens in the previous viewpoint. Hitchens believes that religion causes violence. Do you think violence is perpetuated by religion as Hitchens believes or that the majority of Christians are peaceful, as Volf contends? Why?

Genes May Play a Part in Violent Behavior

Maggie Fox

"These results, which are the first that link molecular genetic variants to delinquency, significantly expand our understanding of delinquent and violent behavior."

In the following viewpoint Maggie Fox says researchers have identified three genes that may play a role in causing violent behavior. According to Fox, researchers at the University of North Carolina studied the genes of violent male juvenile delinquents and found that many of them had three genes in common. Although, the genes appear to be linked to violent behavior, their impact is complex, according to Fox. The researchers found that certain variants of the genes were associated with bad behavior but only when the boys suffered stressful social events, such as failing grades or family issues. The research suggests that genes and environment may work together to cause violence. Fox is a health and science editor for the news service Reuters.

AS YOU READ, CONSIDER THE FOLLOWING QUESTIONS:
  1. Where did the data that was used in the University of North Carolina study come from, according to Fox?
  2. According to Fox, what are the names of the three genes that were associated with bad behavior when the boys suffered stressful events?
  3. According to Fox, what is the name of the gene, which if mutated in a certain way, seemed to set off a young man if he did not have regular meals with his family?

Three genes may play a strong role in determining why some young men raised in rough neighborhoods or deprived families become violent criminals, while others do not, U.S. researchers reported on Monday.

One gene called MAOA that played an especially strong role has been shown in other studies to affect antisocial behavior—and it was disturbingly common, the team at the University of North Carolina reported.

People with a particular variation of the MAOA gene called 2R were very prone to criminal and delinquent behavior, said sociology professor Guang Guo, who led the study.

"I don't want to say it is a crime gene, but 1 percent of people have it and scored very high in violence and delinquency," Guo said in a telephone interview.

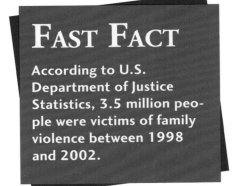

FAST FACT

According to U.S. Department of Justice Statistics, 3.5 million people were victims of family violence between 1998 and 2002.

His team, which studied only boys, used data from the National Longitudinal Study of Adolescent Health, a U.S. nationally representative sample of about 20,000 adolescents in grades 7 to 12. The young men in the study are interviewed in person regularly, and some give blood samples.

Guo's team constructed a "serious delinquency scale" based on some of the questions the youngsters answered.

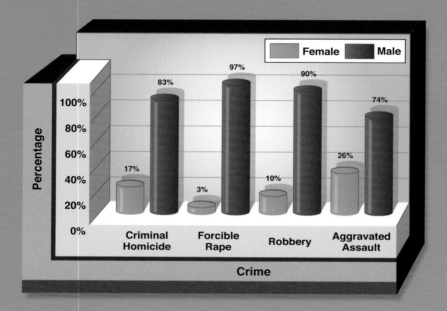

Males Responsible for Most Violent Juvenile Crime in the United States, 2005

Taken from: U.S. Department of Justice, Office of Juvenile Justice and Delinquency Prevention, *Statistical Briefing Book*, 2005.

"Nonviolent delinquency includes stealing amounts larger or smaller than $50, breaking and entering, and selling drugs," they wrote in the August issue of the *American Sociological Review*.

"Violent delinquency includes serious physical fighting that resulted in injuries needing medical treatment, use of weapons to get something from someone, involvement in physical fighting between groups, shooting or stabbing someone, deliberately damaging property, and pulling a knife or gun on someone."

Genes Plus Environment

They found specific variations in three genes—the monoamine oxidase A (MAOA) gene, the dopamine transporter 1 (DAT1) gene and the dopamine D2 receptor (DRD2) gene—were associated with bad behavior, but only when the boys suffered some other stress, such as family issues, low popularity and failing school.

MAOA regulates several message-carrying chemicals called neurotransmitters that are important in aggression, emotion and cognition such as serotonin, dopamine and norepinephrine.

The links were very specific.

Genetic researchers have identified three genes—MAOA, the DAT1 gene, and the DRD2 gene—that are associated with bad behavior.

The effect of repeating a grade depended on whether a boy had a certain mutation in MAOA called a 2 repeat, they found.

And a certain mutation in DRD2 seemed to set off a young man if he did not have regular meals with his family.

"But if people with the same gene have a parent who has regular meals with them, then the risk is gone," Guo said.

"Having a family meal is probably a proxy for parental involvement," he added. "It suggests that parenting is very important."

He said vulnerable children might benefit from having surrogates of some sort if their parents are unavailable.

"These results, which are among the first that link molecular genetic variants to delinquency, significantly expand our understanding of delinquent and violent behavior, and they highlight the need to simultaneously consider their social and genetic origins," the researchers said.

Guo said it was far too early to explore whether drugs might be developed to protect a young man. He also was unsure if criminals might use a "genetic defense" in court.

"In some courts (the judge might) think they maybe will commit the same crime again and again, and this would make the court less willing to let them out," he said.

EVALUATING THE AUTHORS' ARGUMENTS:

In this viewpoint Maggie Fox says that certain genes may be linked to violent behavior in adolescent boys, but only if there are other stressful events in the boys' lives. How might these genetic results be used to support or debunk the previous viewpoints about whether religion causes violence?

Genes Alone Do Not Cause Violence

Sharon Begley

"Even as science identifies the forces that sculpt the mind of a mass killer, explanation is neither excuse nor exculpation. Somewhere in all this is the will, the decision by the gunman to pull the trigger."

In the following viewpoint Sharon Begley contends that violence has no single cause. According to Begley, genes are not enough to create a killer. Neither are brain circuitry, innate personality, environment, or cultural influences. All of these things contribute to violence, says Begley. However, ultimately, the person's free will causes him or her to pull the trigger. Begley is a medical and science writer for the *Wall Street Journal* and *Newsweek*.

AS YOU READ, CONSIDER THE FOLLOWING QUESTIONS:

1. Name two brain chemicals that Begley says the MAOA enzyme breaks down.
2. According to Begley, mass killers are usually in what age range?
3. According to Begley, what percentage of school shooters are suicidal, as reported in a study of school shooters commissioned by the U.S. Department of Education?

Cho Seung-Hui[1] turned his gun on himself before a neuroscientist could get him into a brain-imager and scan his cortex for aberrant activity. No geneticist had analyzed his DNA for genes associated with impulsivity, aggression or violence. And although a physician at a psychiatric hospital concluded in late 2005, after Cho had stalked two female students, that his "affect is flat and mood is depressed," no psychologist had the opportunity to ask him why he wrote such disturbing, demon-haunted plays and essays that his professor referred him for counseling last fall. No sociologist had probed how American society had shaped this 23-year-old South Korean immigrant during his 15 years in the United States.

While the temptation is to dismiss Cho as crazy and leave it at that, no one will ever know for sure why Cho murdered two fellow students in a dormitory at Virginia Tech and then gunned down 30 more people in a classroom building across campus just over two hours later. But the unasked, and perhaps unanswerable, questions show the new sophistication of research on the etiology of violence.

Explaining Violence

Not long ago, scientists invoked genes or brain circuitry, hyper-activity or brutal parental discipline or America's "gun culture" to explain horrors ranging from Charles Whitman's rampage at the University of Texas, Austin, clock tower in 1966, to George Hennard's 23 murders at a Killeen, Texas, diner in 1991, to the Columbine High School shootings in 1999. But although some people with a particular gene variant do grow up to be sociopaths, others with the same variant

---

1. On April 16, 2007, Cho killed and wounded fellow students on the campus of Virginia Polytechnic Institute and State University in Blacksburg, Virginia.

do not. And while some with overactivity in particular regions of the brain commit violent crimes, others do not. And if every kid who became inured to violence through Grand Theft Auto or who witnessed chronic conflict between his parents during early child-hood—risk factors for violence—went on a murder spree, well, then crimes like Cho's wouldn't have network-news anchors rushing to the sites of the massacres to do their broadcasts.

Scientists who study criminal violence—that committed outside of wars and civil conflicts—now believe that its roots are equally planted in the biology of an individual, the psychology that reflects

Virginia Tech shooter Cho Seung-hui was twenty-three years old, but most mass killers are between the ages of twenty-five and thirty-five.

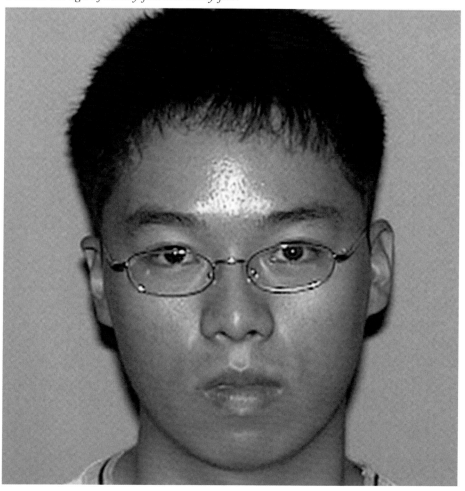

the interaction of innate traits and experiences, and the larger culture. No single cause is sufficient, none is deterministic. "It's like a kid piling up a tower of blocks," says Loyola University, Chicago, psychologist James Garbarino, who has studied school shooters. "Eventually, it falls over. You could point to the final block and say, that one's the cause. But it's an accumulation of risk factors."

Genes Alone Are Not Sufficient

A genetically identical clone of Cho growing up with different experiences in a different environment would likely not have set an American record for mass murder: although the biology would have been sufficiently twisted, the psychology—the product of experiences interacting with that biology—would not have been. Similarly, a Cho who grew up in, say, Japan would almost certainly not have acted on his hatred and fury: biology and psychology set the stage for homicidal violence, but the larger culture would likely have prevented its execution. (Japan is not immune from heinous murders, of course: one day after the Virginia Tech shootings, the mayor of Nagasaki was fatally gunned down on a sidewalk, apparently by a mobster.) What is becoming clear is that criminal violence reflects and requires the dark hand of individual biology, life experiences and the larger cultural surround—and the will to take lives in cold blood.

When behavioral genetics was in its heyday a decade or two ago, one of its grails was a gene predisposing people to violence—and an extended family of Dutch sociopaths seemed to be just what scientists were looking for. Fourteen men in the family had committed impulsive, aggressive crimes including arson and attempted rape. In 1993, scientists reported that all 14 had the identical form of a gene on the X chromosome. The gene makes an enzyme called MAOA [monoamine oxidase A],

> **FAST FACT**
>
> According to the World Health Organization, violence is among the leading causes of death for people aged fifteen to forty-four worldwide, accounting for 14 percent of deaths among males and 7 percent of deaths among females.

which breaks down such brain chemicals as serotonin and noradrenaline. The normal version of the gene produces lots of MAOA; the aberrant form produces low amounts. Studies in animals had linked low enzyme levels to aggression, perhaps because when MAOA is in short supply the brain remains jacked up on neurochemicals in a way that induces aggression.

The "violence gene" theory soon found itself on shaky ground, however. In 2002, scientists who had followed 442 New Zealand men since their birth found that the MAOA link was not nearly as straightforward as the Dutch study suggested. Yes, men with the low-activity form of the MAOA gene were more likely to engage in persistent fighting, bullying, cruelty and violent crime than were men with the high-activity version. But that was so only if they had been neglected or abused as children. If they had not been mistreated, men with the low-activity MAOA gene were not much likelier to be violent. The gene alone was not sufficient. It was not strictly deterministic in the sense of always causing someone to become violent, but merely "permissive": if two boys are severely abused, the one with the low-activity gene is more likely to grow up to commit violent crimes, and even then only if society provides fertile ground for this weed to grow.

Brain Circuitry

The road from genes to behavior travels through the brain. In his research on killers, Adrian Raine of the University of Southern California classifies them as either reactive, those who murder in response to an insult or slight (real or imagined), or proactive, who kill to achieve a thought-out goal such as robbery. Proactive killers show brain-activity patterns no different from that of normal, non-violent volunteers, Raine reported in 1998. But the brains of reactive killers have clearly reduced activity in the prefrontal cortex, the site of such "executive" functions as judgment, planning, abstract reasoning, inhibiting inappropriate or impulsive behavior and self-monitoring. "This is the part of the brain that says, 'Let's stop and think about this again,'" says Raine. "It has a calming effect on the emotional regions of the brain that give rise to pent-up anger and rage." Low prefrontal activity "also means that empathy will be off," says neuropsychiatrist Daniel Amen, who heads a chain of four psychiatric clinics and who found this pattern in the brain of Kip Kinkel, who killed his parents and then shot two dozen fellow students in Springfield, Ore., in 1998 when he was 15. "How do you kill 32 people and have any kind of empathy?" he asks. "That's highly associated with decreased activity in the prefrontal cortex."

In the brains of reactive killers the eerie quiet in the prefrontal regions is paired with increased activity in the limbic regions, site of emotions. "That gives rise to aggression and less prefrontal control over that aggression," Raine says. "It's a sort of double hit that may make them more likely to act out aggressively." Also overactive is a region involved in shifting attention, called the cingulate gyrus. "You become obsessive," Amen says. "Someone with violent thoughts can't let them go. Stalking is one sign of that."

Since the early days of research on the brains of violent felons, how-ever, neuroscience has undergone a paradigm shift. Researchers now know that life experiences and even introspection can alter patterns of brain activity. When people suffering from obsessive-compulsive disorder learn to think about their thoughts differently, for instance, they can quiet activity in the cingulate. That raises the possibility that killers' aberrant brain activity is itself the result of experiences they had or thoughts they thought, rather than something that was wired in at birth. . . .

"It would be so nice if there were a single gene or hormone or neu-rotransmitter or part of the brain that was *it*, the cause, the explana-tion" of violence, [neuroscientist Robert] Sapolsky wrote. But "our behavioral biology is usually meaningless outside the context of the social factors and environment in which it occurs." Which means that the search for the root causes of violence must move up one level, to psychology—the interaction of biology and the life one leads.

Psychological Profile of a Killer

Forensic psychologists have tried to create a profile of a "typical" mass murderer, with some success. More than 90 percent of killers, and even more mass murderers, are male. (Though that may change, just as there are now female suicide bombers in the Mideast.) Mass killers are usually 25 to 35, though school shooters are younger. Few have a serious criminal record. Some kill for revenge, others for fame. Some give off obvious warning signs like Cho's violence-filled writings, others strike unexpectedly. Some kill people they know, others target anyone handy. Rather than being smooth, manipulative psychopaths, says Louis Schlesinger, professor of forensic psychology at the John Jay College of Criminal Justice in New York, mass killers tend to be aggrieved, hurt, clinically depressed, socially isolated and, above all, paranoid.

It is a specific kind of paranoia: a tendency to blame everyone but themselves for their troubles, to believe the world is against them and life is unfair. "They see others as being responsible for their problems; it's never their fault," says James Alan Fox, professor of criminal justice at Northeastern University. "That's why when they come to the decision that life isn't worth living, they decide to take others with them. That's who they hold responsible." In the video he mailed to NBC, Cho rants that "you forced me into a corner and gave me only one option. . . . Now you have blood on your hands that will never wash off." Suggesting counseling is often fruitless. "The response is, 'Counselor? Therapist? I'm the only sane person on campus,'" says sociologist Jack Levin of Northeastern, who last year gave a lecture at Virginia Tech on mass murderers. "They've become so estranged from society, there's nothing you can do short of putting them involuntarily in a psychiatric hospital."

Some mass murderers may be trying to exercise power over a world they believe has left them powerless. "They often feel some great injustice has been done to them. They're angry and they want to take it out on the world," says Schlesinger. "They develop the idea that murder will be the solution to whatever their problem is, and they fixate on it." The problems can range from loss of a job (many office shootings are committed by resentful ex-employees) to a financial setback to a bad breakup. But while such travails may push the killer over the edge, he was teetering there in the first place as a result of a long string of perceived insults, hardships and failed relationships. "You don't just get a D on your report card and then open fire on 30 people," says Levin. "It takes a prolonged series of frustrations. These people are chronically depressed and miserable."

That raises the question of where the misery and the ensuing hatred, resentment and anger come from. An obvious place to look is early childhood. Studies find that up to 45 percent of boys who commit serious violent crimes by the age of 17, and up to 69 percent of girls, were inappropriately aggressive in childhood, picking fights with other kids. It is very rare for violence to show itself for the first time in a person's 20s. (It doesn't work the other way, however. Most aggressive youths mellow out and do not become violent adults, probably because circuits such as those that underlie judgment and impulse control become fully developed only in a person's late teens or early 20s.)

But the link between childhood aggression and later violence is not simply that aggression begets aggression. Instead, an aggressive child, a child with poor impulse control or pathological shyness or even an inability to read other kids' tone of voice elicits certain behaviors and treatment from peers and parents. An odd child cannot make friends. His quirks drive away other kids. He tries his parents patience and love. This back-and-forth between innate tendencies—blame them on genes or on brain wiring, it doesn't matter—magnifies the problematic temperament or behavior and sculpts a psyche that hurtles toward criminal violence. A 2006 study of 334 adolescents found that boys who showed reactive aggression at age 7 had become, by age 16, impulsive, hostile, socially anxious and friendless. Cho was so isolated he barely spoke to roommates, and in the ranting video he sent to NBC, he snarls, "You have vandalized my heart, raped my soul and torched my conscience."

Innate Temperament

Like the discovery that gene expression can depend on the environment, and that brain circuitry reflects life experiences, this, too, is something scientists have only recently nailed down: a child's innate temperament shapes how the world treats him, with the result that that temperament is either reinforced or modified. A child who is innately shy, and who carries genes associated with shyness, can grow up to be as outgoing and socially adept as other kids if her parents encourage that rather than her introversion.

Killers who choose a high-profile crime like Cho's are reaching for one final chance to give their life meaning. "They may think, 'I may never amount to much, but I'm going to die amounting to something. This is my final mark on the world, my final statement,'" says

Jana Martin, a clinical psychologist in Long Beach, Calif. "[Their] fantasy is that they will have the ultimate last word, even if they don't live to see it." The video again: "You thought it was one pathetic boy's life you were extinguishing. Thanks to you, I die like Jesus Christ, to inspire generations of the weak and the defenseless people." Although that reeks of a messianic complex, there is very little research on whether religious belief makes it more likely that someone will resort to mass murder, or less. . . .

Young killers tend to be highly suggestible, modeling their behavior on widely reported crimes. The Columbine shootings inspired several similar plans, and in Cho's video he refers to "martyrs like Eric and Dylan," the Columbine killers. The martyr reference is telling. In the most exhaustive study of school shooters, commissioned by the U.S. Department of Education and the Secret Service after Columbine, researchers examined 37 such cases involving 41 shooters over the previous 25 years. "By the time of the shootings, a good 78 percent of the perpetrators were suicidal," says Harvard University psychologist William Pollack of McLean Hospital. "Those who survived said they wished they'd been killed by the police. They were isolated, felt bullied, harassed. They want to die."

Still, feeling chronically frustrated, blaming others for your problems and being socially isolated are not sufficient to trigger a killing spree. "If everybody in that category were a mass murderer," says Peter Sheras, a clinical psychologist at the University of Virginia, "there would be no one left on the planet." To place the final blocks on the tower and make the whole thing come tragically crashing down, you also need the right environment.

Environment

Barely 24 hours after the Blacksburg murders, Australian Prime Minister John Howard lit into the "gun culture that is such a negative in the United States." That sentiment echoed across the globe and brought a reminder of how Kip Kinkel came to have such easy access to guns. "A psychotherapist actually suggested that his dad buy him a gun so they could have something to do together," says Loyola's Garbarino. "People in other cultures are blown away when they hear that."

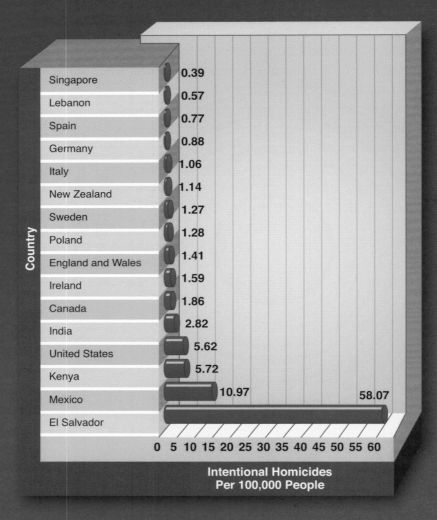

Intentional Homicide Rates in Different Countries, 2006

Country	Intentional Homicides Per 100,000 People
Singapore	0.39
Lebanon	0.57
Spain	0.77
Germany	0.88
Italy	1.06
New Zealand	1.14
Sweden	1.27
Poland	1.28
England and Wales	1.41
Ireland	1.59
Canada	1.86
India	2.82
United States	5.62
Kenya	5.72
Mexico	10.97
El Salvador	58.07

Taken from: United Nations Office on Drugs and Crime, "Tenth United Nations Survey of Crime Trends and Operations of Criminal Justice Systems," 2008.

Guns explain the high body count in Blacksburg and Columbine; you don't hear of many mass stabbings. But historians have long noted the American propensity toward violence independent of the ubiquity of guns. In his 1970 collection *American Violence: A Documentary History,* Richard Hofstadter wrote of the "extraordinary frequency, [the] sheer commonplaceness" of violence in American history. Stanford historian Lawrence Friedman mused that it "must come from somewhere deep in the American personality. . . . The specific facts of American life made it what it is . . . crime has been perhaps a part of the price of liberty."

By the numbers, the United States should have low levels of homicidal violence, which roughly tracks a country's income. Britain, for instance, had 1.5 homicides per 100,000 population between 1998 and 2000. Japan had 1.1, while South Africa had 54. The rate of violent death in the United States was 5.9 per 100,000—above even Turkey's 2.5. Clearly, culture matters. How?

The United States is a nation of immigrants. Those who choose to pull up stakes and try their luck in a distant land "have energy and are willing to take risks," says psychologist John Gartner of Johns Hopkins University. For most immigrants, that translates into a spark and drive that lead them to success in their adopted land. For a few, however, risk-taking coupled with impulsivity may set the stage for violence, Gartner says, "and you do see more violence in immigrant nations like Australia and America." If barriers of language or culture keep an immigrant child from fitting in, it can increase the risk that he will become alienated and, given enough triggers, resort to violence. . . .

As long ago as [nineteenth-century historian and philosopher Alexis de] Tocqueville, observers have divined that the American character had been forged on the frontier. Far from civilization and the reach of laws, we created the cult of the rugged individual who took justice into his own hands. While it's tricky to argue that the "American character" explains a murder spree by a Korean immigrant, living here for 15 impressionable years, Cho could not have avoided soaking in the competitive, individualistic aspects of American culture. "In this country more than others, we admire winners and we blame people for their own inadequacies," says Fox. "Mass murderers tend to be losers, people with a history of failure. The feeling of worthlessness gets internalized" in the barrage of messages that an individual's fate lies entirely in his own hands—something Asian countries view as ludicrous. If success by the usual definition proves elusive, there is another path. The Columbine shooters wrote in their diaries that they needed a certain body count to reach "movie status." In this media-soaked culture, for

Hollywood—or even the most demeaning reality show—to care about your story is the ultimate validation.

The cult of the individual finds its ultimate expression in, yes, America's gun culture. "Guns are the ultimate way of being self-contained and powerful," says Sheras. No matter how the world has treated a potential killer, "if he has a gun he can automatically feel equal to everybody else.". . . .

No discussion of violence in American culture is complete without mentioning blood-soaked videogames. Right after earning points for a graphic disemboweling, young players are more aggressive, but more in punch-little-sister mode than shooting up a mall. Still, there is evidence that violent games have a numbing effect. "When people stop feeling it's terrible that someone is getting hurt, that's dangerous," says Pollack.

The Will

And so the blocks stack up one by one—the biology that mass murderers carry from birth, the brain circuits laid down as they experience life, the messages they soak up from the world around them. No single experience or character trait is sufficient, no single one to blame. But even as science identifies the forces that sculpt the mind of a mass killer, explanation is neither excuse nor exculpation. Somewhere in all this is the will, the decision by the gunman to pull the trigger. Understanding that is the greatest challenge of all.

EVALUATING THE AUTHORS' ARGUMENTS:

Both this viewpoint by Sharon Begley and the previous viewpoint by Maggie Fox refer to the monoamine oxidase A (MAOA) gene. What does each author say about how this gene contributes to violence? Do the authors agree or disagree on the impact this gene has on causing violence? Explain.

Video Games Cause Violence

Anne Harding

"The findings are 'pretty good evidence' that violent video games do indeed cause aggressive behavior."

In the following viewpoint Anne Harding says research links violent video games to violent behavior in adolescent boys. According to Harding, researchers studied boys in Japan and the United States who played certain violent video games and found that after they played the games they were more aggressive. According to Harding, researchers say it is the context and the goal of the violence that matter. Kids should not play video games where the goal is to hunt down and kill people. Anne Harding is a journalist for Health Magazine.

AS YOU READ, CONSIDER THE FOLLOWING QUESTIONS:

1. According to Harding, the researchers from Iowa State University looked at how teens' video game habits at one point in time related to their behavior at what point in the future?
2. According to University of Michigan researcher L. Rowell Huesmann, violent media can spur people to violent actions in two ways. What is the first way?
3. What does Harding say is researcher Cheryl K. Olson's advice to parents about violent video games?

About 90 percent of U.S. kids ages 8 to 16 play video games, and they spend about 13 hours a week doing so (more if you're a boy). Now a new study suggests virtual violence in these games may make kids more aggressive in real life.

Kids in both the U.S. and Japan who reported playing lots of violent video games had more aggressive behavior months later than their peers who did not, according to the study, which appears in the November [2008] issue of the journal *Pediatrics*.

Chicken-or-Egg Problem

The researchers specifically tried to get to the root of the chicken-or-egg problem—do children become more aggressive after playing video games or are aggressive kids more attracted to violent videos? It's a murky—and controversial—issue. Many studies have linked violence in TV shows and video games to violent behavior. But when states have tried to keep under-18 kids from playing games rated "M" for mature, the proposed restrictions have often been challenged successfully in court.

FAST FACT

According to a 2007 Harris poll, 31 percent of male gamers aged eight to eighteen feel "addicted" to video games.

In the new study, Dr. Craig A. Anderson, Ph.D., of Iowa State University in Ames, and his colleagues looked at how children and teens' video game habits at one time point related to their behavior three to six months later.

The study included three groups of kids: 181 Japanese students ages 12 to 15; 1,050 Japanese students aged 13 to 18; and 364 U.S. kids ages 9 to 12. The U.S. children listed their three favorite games and how often they played them. In the younger Japanese group, the researchers looked at how often the children played five different violent video game genres (fighting action, shooting, adventure, among others); in the older group they gauged the violence in the kids' favorite game genres and the time they spent playing them each week. Japanese children rated their own behavior in terms of physical aggression, such as hitting, kicking or getting into fights with other kids; the U.S. children

Entertainment Software Rating Board Rating Symbols

Symbol	Description
EARLY CHILDHOOD **eC** CONTENT RATED BY **ESRB**	**Early Childhood** Titles rated **EC (Early Childhood)** have content that may be suitable for ages 3 and older. Contains no material that parents would find inappropriate.
EVERYONE **E** CONTENT RATED BY **ESRB**	**Everyone** Titles rated **E (Everyone)** have content that may be suitable for ages 6 and older. Titles in this category may contain minimal cartoon, fantasy, or mild violence and/or infrequent use of mild language.
EVERYONE 10+ **E** 10+ CONTENT RATED BY **ESRB**	**Everyone 10+** Titles rated **E10+ (Everyone 10 and older)** have content that may be suitable for ages 10 and older. Titles in this category may contain more cartoon, fantasy or mild violence, mild language and/or minimal suggestive themes.
TEEN **T** CONTENT RATED BY **ESRB**	**Teen** Titles rated **T (Teen)** have content that may be suitable for ages 13 and older. Titles in this category may contain violence, suggestive themes, crude humor, minimal blood, simulated gambling, and/or infrequent use of strong language.
MATURE 17+ **M** CONTENT RATED BY **ESRB**	**Mature** Titles rated **M (Mature)** have content that may be suitable for ages 17 and older. Titles in this category may contain intense violence, blood and gore, sexual content and/or strong language.
ADULTS ONLY 18+ **AO** CONTENT RATED BY **ESRB**	**Adults Only** Titles rated **AO (Adults Only)** have content that should only be played by persons 18 years and older. Titles in this category may include prolonged scenes of intense violence and/or graphic sexual content and nudity.
RATING PENDING **RP** CONTENT RATED BY **ESRB**	**Rating Pending** Titles listed as **RP (Rating Pending)** have been submitted to the ESRB and are awaiting final rating. (This symbol appears only in advertising prior to a game's release).

rated themselves too, but the researchers took into account reports from their peers and teachers as well.

"Pretty Good Evidence"

In every group, children who were exposed to more video game violence did become more aggressive over time than their peers who had less exposure. This was true even after the researchers took into account how aggressive the children were at the beginning of the study—a strong predictor of future bad behavior.

The findings are "pretty good evidence" that violent video games do indeed cause aggressive behavior, says Dr. L. Rowell Huesmann, director of the Research Center for Group Dynamics at the University of Michigan's Institute for Social Research in Ann Arbor.

There are two ways violent media can spur people to violent actions, said Huesmann, who has been studying violence in media and behavior for more than 30 years. First is imitation; children who watch violence in the media can internalize the message that the world is a hostile place, he explains, and that acting aggressively is an OK way to deal with it. Also, he says, kids can become desensitized to violence. "When you're exposed to violence day in and day out, it loses its emotional impact on you," Huesmann said. "Once you're emotionally numb to violence, it's much easier to engage in violence."

But Dr. Cheryl K. Olson, co-director of the Center for Mental Health and the Media at Massachusetts General Hospital in Boston, isn't convinced.

Games Kids Should Definitely Not Be Playing

"It's not the violence per se that's the problem, it's the context and goals of the violence," said Olson, citing past research on TV violence and behavior. There are definitely games kids shouldn't be playing, she said, for example those where hunting down and killing people is the goal. But she argues that the label "violent video games" is too vague. Researchers need to do a better job at defining what is considered a violent video game and what constitutes aggressive behavior, she added.

"I think there may well be problems with some kinds of violent games for some kinds of kids," Olson said. "We may find things we

Researchers in Japan and the United States found that boys who played certain violent video games, such as Grand Theft Auto, were more prone to violence after playing.

should be worried about, but right now we don't know enough." Further, she adds, playing games rated "M" for mature has become "normative behavior" for adolescents, especially boys. "It's just a routine part of what they do," she says.

Her advice to parents? Move the computer and gaming stuff out of kids' rooms and into public spaces in the home, like the living room, so they can keep an eye on what their child is up to.

Dr. David Walsh, president of the National Institute on Media and the Family, a Minneapolis-based non-profit, argues that the pervasiveness of violence in media has led to a "culture of disrespect" in which children get the message that it's acceptable to treat one another rudely and even aggressively. "It doesn't necessarily mean that because a kid plays a violent video game they're immediately going to go out and beat somebody up," Walsh says. "The real impact is in shaping norms, shaping attitude. As those gradually shift, the differences start to show up in behavior."

EVALUATING THE AUTHOR'S ARGUMENTS:

In this viewpoint Anne Harding says that violent video games are linked to violent behavior. Do you think the study cited by Harding is persuasive? Are you convinced that violent video games cause aggressive behavior? How might you design a study to get around the chicken-or-the-egg problem?

Video Games Do Not Cause Violence

Eric DiDomenico

"You can't learn to be a killer through video games."

In the following viewpoint Eric DiDomenico contends that video games do not cause violence. Everyone, he says, wants to blame video games for violence, particularly school shootings, but this is not fair. DiDomenico says children and teens can distinguish fantasy from reality. The perpetrators of the Columbine and Virginia Tech shootings were troubled teens. They may have played video games, but it was the trouble in their lives that caused the shootings, not gaming. DiDomenico believes parents can and should monitor the games their kids play, and society needs to accept gaming as a part of mainstream life. DiDomenico is a computer specialist from Indiana.

AS YOU READ, CONSIDER THE FOLLOWING QUESTIONS:

1. According to DiDomenico, what is the name of the song that was inspired partly by the Columbine killings? What is the name of the band who released the song?
2. What is the name of the game DiDomenico's niece Meghan likes to play?
3. What is "edutainment," according to DiDomenico?

"**N**obody shoots anybody in the face unless you're a hit man or a video gamer." Those are the words spoken by Jack Thompson, a lawyer from the state of Florida. Jack Thompson, in broad strokes, declared that if you buy games such as the Grand Theft Auto series and first person shooters like Counterstrike and Quake III Arena, you're going to be a terrorist, murderer, or a crime thug in the future.

Nothing can be further from the truth. Children at the tender age of seven can be easily taught the difference between fantasy and reality by their parents or another adult; and sometimes kids learn the two aforementioned ideals on their own. Teenagers are no different from children, except when reaching puberty, their bodies go through a physical change and their tempers can flare easily. Children fight just as much as teenagers.

Teenagers are bullied by their peers just as much as children are. Children usually tell grown-ups when they've been tormented. When going through puberty, teenagers are at an imbalanced stage. Many youths do get help from parents and teachers. And some aggressors get a joy out of aggravating their quarry that they don't stop, even when ordered to do so, because it makes them God.

Troubled Teens

And then there are some teenagers who are just always told to let it roll off of their back and forget about it, regardless of the number of times they've been attacked; these are the teenagers that are, by no fault of their own, at greater risk. Regardless of gender, everyone has their breaking point. No matter how many times people are told to ignore the "bad apples," they will eventually be pushed too far. By then, it's too little, far, far too late.

Take for example, April 20, 1999: the Columbine High Massacre. Eric Harris and Dylan Klebold were two students that killed nearly fifteen students and injuring nearly twenty more before they committed suicide in the library of the school.

There has been much speculation that social cliques were part of the school and the two individuals could not find a place to fit in, making them feel insecure, depressed, and desperate for attention. Probably to them, everyone considered them freaks and out of the

The band P.O.D. performs their song "Youth of a Nation" on the Tonight Show. *The song was inspired by the Columbine shootings and is about troubled youth.*

norm. Like me, all they knew was gaming. Police reports released several years after the events . . . show the two students were mentally unstable before the slaughter.

Why these reports were not brought to the attention of the public for so long has not been disclosed. But even then, the public still blamed it all on the games they played such as Doom. Harris had created many maps to the Doom game and released them on the web [site] known as the Harris Files. Shortly after Harris and Klebold "snapped," Harris used mod tools, or better known as modification tools, within the Doom game to create a map bearing a strong resemblance to the Columbine High school to plot how he and Klebold would commence their killing spree.

This is an example of when grown-ups around should've realized that the two troubled students needed help. Once again . . . too late.

The band P.O.D. released a song called "Youth of the Nation," which was partly inspired by the events of the killings [and] is about many troubled youths; some would live in obscurity, others would "let the world know how they feel with the sound of a cap." In my opinion, everyone needs to listen to the song.

Blaming Video Games

Flash forward to April 16, 2007, the day of the Virginia Tech Massacre. The perpetrator this time was a South Korean named Seung-hui Cho. After the events of the shootings, Jack Thompson came forth and said Cho had played the game Counterstrike since being in Virginia Tech and the game taught him how to be nothing more than a murderer.

The police searched Cho's belongings and his computer, but the game was never found, indicating Cho had not played it; thus this is another piece of proof of video games being blamed. But what many people overlooked until after the police disclosed their findings was Cho was another unstable individual with an anxiety disorder called selective mutism and suffered from depression.

Many have said he was too quiet and didn't socialize much. Medical records and testimonies from his family said he'd been troubled with his illnesses since he was merely a child. I don't want to say he was a troubled youth throughout his life. It was clear from the beginning he needed help. He was given help, but it was not through the proper treatment methods.

A judge ruled that Cho was a danger to himself and to others and needed immediate help. He was detained at a hospital, but was only treated as an outpatient and not as a committed patient, thus the extent of his illnesses were unknown. Because of this, he was still allowed under Virginia Law to buy weapons. Another example of "too late." The failure wasn't the fault of games, it was the fault of the people around Cho.

I have no pity and feel none for the shooters. I only feel sorrow for them and their victims.

The school shootings mentioned above are prime examples that you can't learn to be a killer through video games. If one were to use these games to plot out his or her "revenge," then the individual is past the point of no return. But just because people create a game map of the school they attend doesn't also mean they're going to shoot someone. We need to be more observant of other people, especially our children.

Not Considered "Mainstream"

Video games are like movies, books, and music: they're another form of entertainment. But the main reason games are being blamed for school violence is primarily because games are just a hobby. Video

Who Plays What?

2004 Computer and Video Game Sales by Rating
by Units Sold

Taken from: Entertainment Software Association, *Essential Facts About the Computer and Video Game Industry*, 2005.

games, unlike movies, books, and music, are not yet ingrained into our culture.

They're not considered mainstream. State governors and legislators have always signed a law banning minors from buying mature-rated games. And in turn the ESA, or the Entertainment Software Association, has appealed these laws, causing the laws to be shot down or overturned and considered illegal. I do applaud the government's trying to look out for young children, but I don't agree with their practices such as preventing young children from getting their hands on mature content.

Parents Should Decide

Honestly, this is the responsibility of the parent. If a child wants to buy a game and it's rated mature, then the parents have the right to ask a store clerk to pop it in and watch their child play. As they play the game, the parents can then study the content and decide whether the game is acceptable for their kid.

They can also look at the rating on the front of the box and on the back of the game for the reasons of the game's rating. I'm a twenty-six-year-old uncle with two nieces, and the majority of games I play are Teen-rated and Mature-rated, though I do play a lot of games that are rated "E" for Everyone.

My oldest niece, Meghan, likes to play a game called Halo: Combat Evolved with me. The game is mature-rated but I have played through the game to know that it is suitable for her. The reasons for the mature rating in the Halo games are because of blood and mild-to-moderate language. There are no body parts flying off of people or aliens, so there is no level of gore, just a healthy amount of blood. If the game had vulgar language, such as language you'd hear in a prison like the game The Suffering, and had no option to censor some of the words, I wouldn't let her play.

Meghan is not squeamish when it comes to blood, but she knows the blood is in the game to show attention to detail; thus she has a firm grasp on the concept of violence. She also likes to play Tom Clancy's Splinter Cell: Chaos Theory; in this game you play as a government agent to preserve and keep the U.S. safe from terrorist attacks. It's also mature rated and has moments of strong language, but those moments in the Single Player mode are very rare and nonexistent in the Cooperative Play mode. She wanted to play Splinter Cell: Double Agent, and it was like SC: Chaos Theory, but there were moments I felt the game was too dark and gritty to allow her to play it.

Video Games Are Educational

Believe it or not, games like the above-mentioned have a thing called a story, and it's what drives people to play the game. Some games have a story already told in the manual, but other games conceal the story within the game and the story unfolds as the game is played. Deus Ex and Deus Ex: Invisible War are two popular examples of story-driven game play.

But alas some adults, members of the media, and politicians don't think of the aforementioned and often blame the problems of our youth on the form of entertainment called video gaming. Believe it or not, there are some video games that are educational for both parents and adults; these games have a category called Edutainment, or educational entertainment. A TV channel called the Discovery Channel has shows about animals and gives fun facts about these creatures, thus placing them in the Edutainment category. But gaming is not yet considered part of our society, thus fingers are pointed at games.

Focus on Real Problems, Not Simulated Ones

We need to wake up to the fact that games are going to eventually be a part of our lives down the road instead of making them the cause of all our problems. If you kill people in a game, you're just killing a character made out of polygons. If you die, you can restart your game. There's no reset button in real life: if you kill a person, there are going to be serious consequences for doing so; and if you kill yourself, you're gone.

Bottom line: we need to make sure there are other causes of our children becoming violent such as mental health and bullying. We can't baby our children, but we do need to know when to step in and help them. The real war is on life's issues, not fantasy people in a simulated environment.

EVALUATING THE AUTHORS' ARGUMENTS:

In this viewpoint Eric DiDomenico contends that video games do not cause violence. What evidence does he use to support his contention? What is the difference between the evidence DiDomenico uses and the evidence Anne Harding used to support the previous viewpoint? Which evidence do you think is stronger and why?

Chapter 2

Is Violence Necessary?

Many feel that people worldwide are increasingly relying on violence to make their opinions heard.

Violence Is a Part of Human Nature

Wes Heinkel

"War is inevitable; murder is not anomalous; both are [part of] the human condition."

In the following viewpoint Wes Heinkel argues that violence is a part of human nature. He contends that murders, such as those that occurred at Virginia Tech in 2007, are a by-product of the human condition, and as such, they will never go away. It is wrong to believe that this aspect of human nature can be changed, says Heinkel. War and murder are a part of being human. Heinkel is a writer for the *Western Courier*, a student-run newspaper serving Western Illinois University.

AS YOU READ, CONSIDER THE FOLLOWING QUESTIONS:

1. What does Heinkel say has been the human cliché since our conception?
2. What reason does Heinkel give for the Virginia Tech shooter's vehement opposition to "rich kids"?
3. According to Heinkel, who said violent actions are "human nature just being what it is"?

The tragic events that occurred at Virginia Tech last week [April 16, 2007] provided a depressing and un-idealistic account of the fundamental problem with our species: human nature.

Over time, our species has proved to be the most intelligent and yet irrational to ever grace, for lack of a better word, this blue planet we call Earth. The technological advances and standard of living we have achieved in a relatively short time undoubtedly solidifies our position at the top of the food chain.

Our ability to adapt, persevere and then conquer any adversary or problem we deem worthy is one of our greatest assets. From medicine to space to physics, we have broken through barriers time and again and will continue to do so as long as we exist.

Human Nature Always Beckons

However, throughout our various advances and thorough understanding of things the way they are, human nature has always and will continue to beckon our hearts and minds. And although it has brought many fruitful endeavors, it will ultimately lead to murder, chaos, genocide, extermination, anarchy, war and the prominent but very destructive struggle for power.

"'Devour to survive" has been the human cliché since our conception. Thus we have harnessed the destructive dominance of atoms first

A scene from a movie illustrates the point that the human propensity toward violence began early in the evolutionary process.

through fission and then through fusion, producing weaponry that can incinerate flesh and bone in less than a millisecond.

On a smaller scale, we design bullets that are meant to tumble through the body after penetrating flesh and leave an exit wound four times greater than the size of the entry for maximum killing capacity. As technology has advanced, human nature has remained static; in other words, technology has only exacerbated our proficiency to take life.

The late and influential writer Kurt Vonnegut discussed the absurdities of war and the dehumanizing effects it has on the psyches, minds and hearts of people in his various books, most notably in *Slaughterhouse Five*. Despite being an anti-war advocate, Vonnegut, through his disjointed plots and science fiction, understood the inevitability of war and its catalyst—human nature.

Shooting Was By-Product of Human Condition

Many professional psychologists and psychiatrists and various people in the medical field will say the young man [student Cho Seung-hui] responsible for the 32 dead and several wounded at Virginia Tech was insane, depressed, socially unaccepted—whatever suits their fancy. But the fact is, the brain is separate from the mind, and what transpired at Virginia Tech was a by-product of the human condition. Because of its cause, it will happen again in one form or another.

This man—I'm not justifying his actions, for tragedies like this cannot be justified—was rendered powerless, causing him to go on a quest to get whatever it was that he lost back. The shooter vehemently opposed the "rich kids," as seen in the letters and film. Why do [you] think that is? He felt less powerful to them and in many ways less important.

Human nature, for better or worse, dictates the history and future of mankind. In the liberal bubble of college academia, you

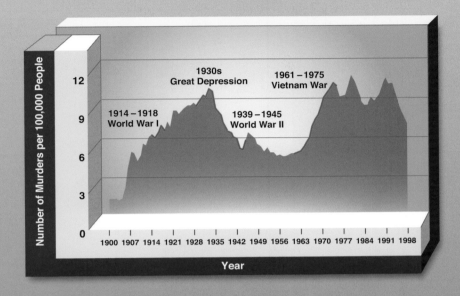

United States Murder Rate, 1900–1998

Number of Murders per 100,000 People

12

9

6

3

0

1930s
Great Depression

1961–1975
Vietnam War

1914–1918
World War I

1939–1945
World War II

1900 1907 1914 1921 1928 1935 1942 1949 1956 1963 1970 1977 1984 1991 1998

Year

Taken from: Justice Research and Statistics Association, *Crime and Justice Atlas 2000.*

are going to have a lot of hopeless intellectuals inject idealism into your veins. In hopes to provide a world free from war, murder, tyranny and evil, yet in actuality they do you and me an incredible disservice.

Their intentions are good, but sometimes "The best laid plans of mice and men often go awry." Their ill-fated attempt to console or give us the false belief that we have control over ancient mysteries like human nature, war and the never-ending struggle for power may cause us to overlook what we really are, and more importantly, what we are capable of.

Violence Inevitable

War is inevitable; murder is not anomalous; both are [part of] the human condition: The actions of the young man at Virginia Tech are, as [Greek historian] Thucydides said, "human nature just being what it is." Depressing? Yes. But we should expect and prepare for more of the same. Conditions similar to those which resulted in the VT shooting will continue to rise and human life will again be placed in jeopardy because the most brutal elements of our nature will always resurface and be acted upon.

EVALUATING THE AUTHOR'S ARGUMENTS:

In this viewpoint Wes Heinkel says violence is a part of human nature and cannot be changed. What other things do you think are a part of human nature? Do you think human nature can change in general? Do you think the violent aspect of human nature can be changed, and if so, how?

Viewpoint 2

Violence Is Not Necessarily a Part of Human Nature

Clara Moskowitz

"Human nature is compatible with a peaceful existence."

In the following viewpoint Clara Moskowitz asserts that violence may not be an unchangeable part of human nature. According to Moskowitz, many scientists believe that we are not destined for continual human violence; the peaceful utopia depicted in *Star Trek* movies could occur. Moskowitz also says that many peaceful cultures already exist here on Earth. Moskowitz writes about astronomy and space. She has written for *Wired,* Space.com, LiveScience.com, and other sources.

AS YOU READ, CONSIDER THE FOLLOWING QUESTIONS:

1. According to Dennis Fox, if utopia does come it will be because of what?
2. According to Richard Koenigsberg, warfare is linked to the human attachment to what?
3. What examples of current peaceful societies does the author provide?

Tricorders and transporters are cool, but the most radical invention on *Star Trek* may have been its vision of a peaceful humanity.

Sure, humans are always getting into fights on the show's original and spin-off series, but generally with other, less "enlightened" alien species. Earth in the *Star Trek* universe is an egalitarian, utopian planet that has long ago shrugged off the habit of war. People in *Star Trek*'s vision of the 23rd century use their time and talents to explore the universe, create art and probe the mysteries of science. Sounds nice, huh?

While some have dismissed this aspect of the show as its most fanciful element, psychologists and political scientists say it might not be so unrealistic. "I do think humans might someday reach more peaceful coexistence if we don't destroy the planet first, though I doubt it will be utopia," said Dennis Fox, emeritus professor of legal studies and psychology at the University of Illinois at Springfield. "If utopia does come, it won't be because human nature changes, or because some governmental authority or alien race forces it upon us, but because we manage to create new social structures more conducive to satisfying human needs and values."

War and Peace Begin in the Mind

Human nature is compatible with a peaceful existence, Fox and other psychologists say.

An international group of 20 scientists convened in Seville, Spain, in 1986 by the Spanish National Commission for UNESCO [United Nations Educational, Scientific, and Cultural Organization] came to the same conclusion. "Just as 'wars begin in the minds of men,' peace also begins in our minds. The same species who invented war is capable of inventing peace," the group wrote in its *Seville Statement on Violence*.

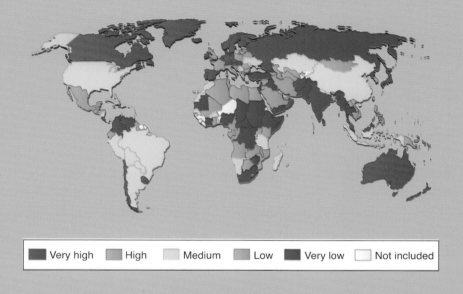

Global Peace Index 2009

Very high █ High █ Medium █ Low █ Very low ☐ Not included

Taken from: Institute for Economics and Peace, Economist Intelligence Unit, www.visionofhumanity.org/gpi/home.php, 2009.

Not everyone agrees, though. Some scientists say aggression is a fundamental human trait built into us by thousands of years of evolution.

A 2008 study published in the journal *Psychopharmacology* found that when mice display aggression, their brains are rewarded with dopamine, a pleasure-inducing neurotransmitter. The findings are thought to extend to humans. "We learned from these experiments that an individual will intentionally seek out an aggressive encounter solely because they experience a rewarding sensation from it," said study leader Craig Kennedy, professor of pediatrics at Vanderbilt University in Tennessee.

Maybe both peace and violence are part of human nature, some say. "Humans are wired with great potentials for altruism, caring and compassion but also for destructive competition and for killing," said Marc Pilisuk, a psychologist at Saybrook Graduate School and Research Center in San Francisco.

Governments and Nations May Be to Blame

Besides human nature, the main hurdle to peace is bad government, some scientists say.

"A better world, if it comes into being, depends not so much on technological fixes as on breaking down centers of power so that we can all play a significant role in deciding matters that affect our daily lives," Fox told SPACE.com.

Pilisuk agrees. "If there is a common enemy around which humanity can unite, it is the institutions that protect privilege for an elite network with extraordinary power and minimal accountability," Pilisuk wrote in an e-mail. "At present, hopes for peace look most promising in the decentralized myriad of creative local actions of people wanting leaders to respond to their true needs."

Taking this idea a step further, Richard Koenigsberg, a former professor of psychology at Queens College in New York City, argues that it's not governments, but the idea of countries at all that creates war. "Warfare is linked to the human attachment to 'nations.' As long as people believe that countries are the most significant thing in the world and that 'nations have the right to kill,' then warfare will persist," he said.

Perhaps if humans come to see ourselves as residents of a single planet, rather than citizens of individual nations with specific interests, war will be unnecessary. "War is not part of human nature," Koenigsberg told SPACE.com. "It is intimately linked to our psychic attachment to countries."

Already Peace on Earth?

Hope for a nonviolent society might not have to wait until the 23rd century. Peace on Earth already exists in some places.

"Although our own society has a good deal of violence, there are societies which are pretty nonviolent—no wars and very few murders and rapes—and they are not fighting aliens," said psychologist Joseph de Rivera, director of the Peace Studies Program at Clark University in Massachusetts.

The Web site Peacefulsocieties.org lists current and past nonviolent societies. Examples include the Batek people of Malaysia, the Himalayan Buddhist Ladakhi people, The Mbuti rainforest-dwellers

The Batek people of Malaysia are an example of small, nonviolent human societies.

of Central Africa, and even the American Amish. These communities have found ways to resolve conflicts without war, so maybe the rest of us can, too.

"I'm hopeful for two reasons," de Rivera said. "1.) Most people don't like to be dominated by the powerful. 2.) Although we don't have aliens to fight against we do have nasty viruses and global warming that we have to unify to deal with."

There's nothing like a really big problem to bring people together.

EVALUATING THE AUTHORS' ARGUMENTS:

In this viewpoint Clara Moskowitz asserts that peace on Earth is possible. In the previous viewpoint Wes Heinkel contends that it is not. What do you think: Is peace on Earth possible? Why or why not? What would you do to bring about peace on Earth?

The Christian Just War Doctrine Allows Violence

Edward J. McBride

"*It remains of the utmost importance to realize that the legitimacy, justness, and righteousness of the decision to wage war are all of a piece. They are neither separable nor hierarchically arranged.*"

In the following viewpoint Edward J. McBride explains the "just war" doctrine. According to the author, the just war doctrine is presented and fully described in the catechism of the Catholic Church. Though many presume that Catholics, indeed most Christians, are opposed to war, the just war theory maintains that a decision to wage war is legitimate, as long as the war has a morally just goal that is for the common good. Edward J. McBride is an emeritus professor of political science at St. Mary's University in Halifax, Nova Scotia.

AS YOU READ, CONSIDER THE FOLLOWING QUESTIONS:
1. According to the article, what historical figure has been given credit for forming the framework for the just war doctrine of today?
2. According to the information McBride presents, what are the three conditions for a just war?
3. According to the author, what kind of obligation does public authority have?

"The aim of any ruler should be to promote the welfare of the territory that he has been given to rule."

— St. Thomas Aquinas, De Regimine Principum, Chapter 2.

"Catholic teaching begins in every case with a presumption against war." While such a declaration appeals to a commendable pacific inclination, it distorts the traditional Catholic principles of war and peace. Catholic Just War Doctrine, based on Catholic political thought, inextricably intertwines order, justice, and peace.

Canadian Bishops

The Canadian Conference of Catholic Bishops, in a statement issued on January 17, 2003, presumptively discountenanced the very notion of a war against Saddam Hussein's regime in Iraq. This is their choice and right. One would not welcome a "naked public square" devoid of politico-moral comments by men of the cloth. What would be welcome, though, is some recognizable consonance between the views expressed and the religious tradition ostensibly represented.

If the bishops deserve attentive hearing, then so does the traditional Catholic Just War theory. Chief among its shaping influences are Saint Thomas Aquinas and Saint Augustine. Neither entertains any presumption against war, per se. Instead, both maintain that war must have a telos, an end or goal morally proper to the enterprise.

Just War Teaching

Set in broader context, that goal is the objective of political association itself—"the common good," which remains the particular responsibility of "the one who has care of the community." Saint Thomas Aquinas delineates the moral dictates for the decision to wage war as follows:

> There are three conditions for a just war. First, the ruler under whom the war is to be fought must have authority. . . . Secondly, a just cause is required—so that those against whom war is waged deserve such a response because of some offence on their part. The third condition that is required on the part of those making the war is a right intention, to achieve some good or avoid some evil.

Aquinas expands upon these three conditions in the following passages. First, regarding the requisite legitimate authority, he writes:

> Since the responsibility for the commonwealth has been entrusted to rulers it is their responsibility to defend the city or kingdom or province subject to them. And just as it is legitimate for them to use the material sword to punish criminals in order to defend it against internal disturbances . . . so they also have the right to use the sword of war to defend the commonwealth against external enemies.

Second, by regarding the requisite just cause, Aquinas quotes Augustine:

> Just wars are usually defined as those that avenge injuries, when a nation or city should be punished for failing to right a wrong done by its citizens, or to return what has been taken away unjustly.

Right Intention

Third, Aquinas again quotes Augustine to telling effect:

> For the true followers of God even wars are peaceful if they are waged not out of greed or cruelty but for the sake of peace, to restrain the evildoers and assist the good.

Initially, it is important to characterize properly the above precepts. They are not heuristic exercises designed for abstract philosophical inquiry. They are principled canons for the actual conduct of statecraft.

Authority

As a case in point, the fact that Aquinas first addresses the need for competent authority is of appreciable significance. What then follows is not an admonition to avoid war at all cost. Rather, what ensues under the just cause and right intention categories is a reminder that duly constituted

public authority has the moral obligation to preserve and defend the common good. Avenging injuries to the commonweal, righting wrongs, restraining and punishing evildoers, returning things unjustly seized—these are all constituents, operationally considered, of that public good.

It remains of the utmost importance to realize that the legitimacy, justness, and righteousness of the decision to wage war are all of a piece. They are neither separable nor hierarchically arranged. They are, at one and the same time, reciprocally clarifying, qualifying, and enabling.

Task of Discerning

The public authority entrusted with promoting the common good must determine if "some offence" warrants recourse to war against the offender, and must intend "to achieve some good or avoid some evil." The offence deserving of a belligerent response is not confined to direct aggression, nor is the right intention reduced to that of repelling such aggression. To borrow a term from constitutional jurisprudence, this stands as "the original understanding" of the Catholic Just War doctrine.

With the passage of time, "the original understanding" has undergone both accretion and deletion, and has become somewhat over-schematized. None of these developments, one is prepared to argue, has been particularly constructive. Taken together, one would further contend, they have contributed to making a muddle of "the original understanding."

The Universal Catechism

These changes, especially in combination, both reflect and shape the claim that "Catholic teaching begins in every case with presumption against war." For an apt illustration—perhaps altogether too apt—one need look no further than the 1992 Catechism of the Catholic Church. The relevant entries (#2307–2317), subject the classic Just War Doctrine to accretion, deletion, and schematic distortion.

All citizens and all governments are obliged to work for the avoidance of war. However, "as long as the danger of war persists and there is no international authority with the necessary competence and power, governments cannot be denied the right of lawful self-defence, once all peace efforts have failed." The thematic statement in the Catechism on the subject bespeaks the functional equivalent of a presumption against war: "all citizens and all governments are obliged to work for the avoidance of war" (# 2308). This pronouncement then immediately becomes one of those "Yes, but" propositions so familiar to political scientists: "However, as long as the danger of war persists and there is no international authority. . . ."

In an interesting accretion, "all citizens," now accorded first mention, have the obligation "to work for the avoidance of war." How this would take effect in countries where the people are really enslaved subjects, rather than citizens, is left unsaid. The Catechism remains similarly silent on the practical aspects of this role even for citizens in a free and democratic society.

The section next (# 2309), presents a compendium of constraints upon the commencement and conduct of war. There is a preface, followed by an undifferentiated checklist of restrictions:

- The strict conditions for *legitimate defence by military force* (emphasis in the original) require rigorous consideration. The gravity of such a decision makes it subject to rigorous conditions of moral legitimacy. At one and the same time:

- the damage inflicted by the aggressor on the nation or community of nations must be *lasting, grave, and certain* (emphasis mine);

- all other means of putting an end to it must have been shown to be impractical or ineffective;

- there must be serious prospects of success;

- the use of arms must not produce evils and disorders graver than the evil to be eliminated. The power of modern means of destruction weighs very heavily in evaluating this condition.

These constraints are freighted with language that would purportedly raise the rhetorical bar against war. That a portion of a catechism would assume an admonitory tone hardly represents anything unusual. To whom, though, are the admonitions addressed? Equally to the "all citizens and all governments" of #2308? Alas, some peoples and some leaders are more equal than others in accepting moral guidance for the waging of war.

In brief, the receptive constituency for #2309 seems confined to constitutional democracies. Moreover, even such countries would find it foolhardy—before responding to an aggressor—to sustain "damage" that is "lasting, grave, and certain." That might well prove a formula for defeat that itself is "lasting, grave, and certain."

Section #2309 concludes with two statements, both of which are problematic—albeit for different reasons. The first of these summarizes in this fashion: "These are the *traditional elements* enumerated in what is called the 'just war' doctrine" (emphasis mine). In light of the Augustinian and Thomistic views already cited, one can only respond in the words of a certain car-rental commercial, "Not exactly."

The final sentence of #2309 notes that "The evaluation of these conditions for moral legitimacy belongs to the prudential judgment of those who have responsibility for the common good." Just so, but the placement at the end of the analysis inverts the order of the Thomistic approach. The latter beings with the duty of the ruler to determine whether "those against whom war is waged deserve such a response because of some offence on their part." The priority proposition of Aquinas counsels that the ruler be cognizant of the duty chiefly to counter action inimical to the common good. The seeming afterthought of the Catechism implies that those in authority have the responsibility mainly to implement the restrictions that it imposes.

Safeguarding Peace

If the above inversion is a schematic distortion that causes some difficulty, then the Catechism also contains an even more vexing one. The sections that precede the topic of war are devoted to the subject of peace (#2303–2306); under "peace" the Catechism, quoting Augustine, incisively calls peace "the tranquility of order." It extends this sound thought by concluding that "Peace is the work of Justice and the effect of Charity." Again just so, but the war sections that follow never mention the interconnection as adduced by Aquinas and Augustine of an "order of justice" (Aquinas), an "order of peace" (Augustine), and the love of both that can bestow upon war a "justice transformed" by charity. (Aquinas).

The Allied release of Germany from the iron grip of the Nazi regime in World War II exemplifies the previous quote from Augustine: ". . . Wars are peaceful if they are waged not out of greed or cruelty but for the sake of peace, to restrain the evildoers and assist the good." Furthermore, Aquinas subsumed the obligation of soldiers in a just war under the heading of charity. When a war is righteous, according to Aquinas, combatants should fight out of love for both justice and their countrymen. What is more, the Angelic Doctor [an honorific title for Aquinas] even exempts the soldier from not intending to kill in self-defence.

However, because killing is only allowed by action of public authority for the common good, it is not lawful for someone who is acting in self-defence to intend to kill another man—except for those who in the exercise of public authority justify the act of self-defence as related to the public good. This is the case with a soldier fighting against the enemy.

This scarcely seems the language and reasoning of "a presumption against war."

Parenthetically, the Catechism of the Catholic Church is a treasury of orthodoxy, richly allusive to the doctrinal patrimony of the Church. The present writer has copiously drawn upon it in teaching high school catechism for his parish. The criticism found in this article applies solely to its specific topic.

North American Bishops

It appears logical, *in fine* [in the end], that a few provisions in the 1992 Catechism are less cause, and more effect, of any jumbled just

Civilian Death Rates Rise in Iraq After U.S.-Led Invasion

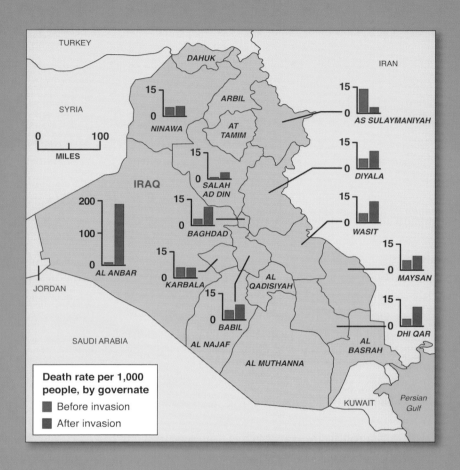

Taken from: Rob Stein, "100,000 Civilian Deaths Estimated in Iraq," *Washington Post*, October 29, 2004. www.washingtonpost.com/wp-srv/nation/daily/graphics/civilian_102904.gif. *Lancet*.

war theory. By the same token, debate over war in Iraq has only highlighted, but hardly determined, the incoherent state of Catholic reasoning on war and peace. North American Catholic episcopal pronouncements serve to demonstrate the point. First, there was an attribution to the American bishops of a "statement that the U.S. has a moral right and duty to defend the common good against aggression." This, however, was soon undercut: "Based on the facts that are known to us, we continue to find it difficult to meet the strict Catholic teaching for overriding the strong presumption against the use of military force."

The White House's response was to inform the bishops and other non Catholic clergymen whom they joined that "the president will respect their thoughts, and he will act as he sees fit as commander-in-chief." The Canadian Catholic Bishops' contribution need not detain us, since it actually had nothing whatsoever to do with the just war doctrine, either original or revised.

It is instructive, perhaps, to borrow again from constitutional jurisprudence. If the original Just War Doctrine were a constitutional provision, then it would be regarded as having undergone substantial amendment. Is this better than before? It is debatable, but the question is not under argument here. Is the current amalgamated version coherent? That question is under argument here. The classic doctrine has not been repealed, only amended. Some can still cite "the original understanding," while others can turn to the revision. More importantly, each side can claim a Catholic provenance for its views. In this hybrid doctrine, its older and newer elements are more than merely distinguishable. They so differ in style and content as to yield different results in their actual application.

The Classic View

The classic view represents a warrant of authority to those charged with the common good to employ war as an instrument of that public trust. It principally demands that the recourse to military force be exercised according to due cause, by duly constituted and empowered caretakers of the common good. Augustine and Aquinas would have the war power manifest an authoritative character, that is, its exercise has to be objectively referrable to the common good. The revisionist view is a vehicle of criticism to which private citizens can repair in questioning the war plans of the responsible officers of government. It principally demands that the resort to war be exercised according to a series of tests designed to demonstrate its validity to the interested public. The altered Catholic Just War Doctrine would have the ward power manifest a probative quality, namely, its rationale has to be susceptible of virtual proof.

Given the bifurcation of the Catholic viewpoint on war, "sentire cum ecclesia" (thinking with the Church), has become increasingly difficult. It might ease the difficulty by bringing the two strands into a reorganized and, one hopes, more coherent schema. This remains a task best deferred to a less clamorous time.

EVALUATING THE AUTHORS' ARGUMENTS:

In this viewpoint, McBride contends that war is justified in the face of evil and with the correct intentions. What other viewpoint is based on a similar contention with the one presented? Do you think people can have different opinions on whether a war is just or not? Explain.

Christians Should Always Promote Nonviolence

Ken Butigan

"As Christians, our faith calls us now more than ever to join with one another to take powerful nonviolent resistance to end war."

In the following viewpoint Ken Butigan asserts that there are no "just wars," and Christians should join together to end all violence. According to Butigan, since the time of Jesus, Christians have practiced non-violent resistance. Jesus himself espoused it in teachings such as "turn the other cheek" and "give your cloak if someone takes your coat." Butigan believes Christians should actively promote nonviolent resistance in the wake of the September 11 attacks and the war on terror. Ken Butigan is the executive director of Pace e Bene, a worldwide organization dedicated to nonviolence and building a more peaceful world.

AS YOU READ, CONSIDER THE FOLLOWING QUESTIONS:
1. Butigan uses India's independence and Aung San Suu Kyi's democracy movement in Burma as examples of "people power" and nonviolent resistance. In addition to these, what other examples does he provide?

Ken Butigan, "The Spiritual Journey of Christian Nonviolent Resistance," *Response Magazine*, November 2002. Reproduced by permission. Ken Butigan is director of Pace e Bene Nonviolence Service and is on the faculty of DePaul University's Peace, Justice and Conflict Resolution Program in Chicago, IL.

2. According to Butigan, what is the name of the scripture scholar who refers to "the myth of redemptive violence?"
3. Who wrote, "They need brigades of ambulance drivers who will have to ignore the red lights of the present system until the emergency is solved," according to Butigan?

From the time of the biblical story of the Hebrew midwives who committed the first recorded act of civil disobedience by refusing to carry out Pharaoh's order to kill Hebrew babies, to the innumerable movements for nonviolent change taking place around the globe today, human beings have used the power of active, creative, audacious and relentlessly persistent nonviolence to change themselves, their communities and their world. As Christians, our faith calls us now more than ever to join with one another to take powerful nonviolent resistance to end war, to fashion economic and racial justice, to protect the earth and to champion the well-being and inclusion of all.

What Is Nonviolent Resistance?

Nonviolent resistance, broadly defined, is a form of embodied social change that actively and persistently challenges violent and unjust conditions, structures or policies through non-injurious means. It is the process in which "people power"—the power of ordinary people—is mobilized to withdraw support from unjust policies and to create the moral and political conditions for change by "leading the leaders." The following recent example conveys the power and importance of such nonviolence in action.

Nigeria is the world's sixth largest oil producer and the United States' fifth largest supplier, yet many Nigerians do not share in this teeming wealth. Intent on changing this disparity, this summer [2004] hundreds of unarmed Nigerian women of the Ugborodo and Arutan communities dramatically occupied ChevronTexaco's key oil terminal in the country, bringing petroleum production to a sudden halt. After ten dramatic days, the women reached a landmark pact with the company to provide jobs, infrastructure, and economic empowerment in villages long mired in poverty.

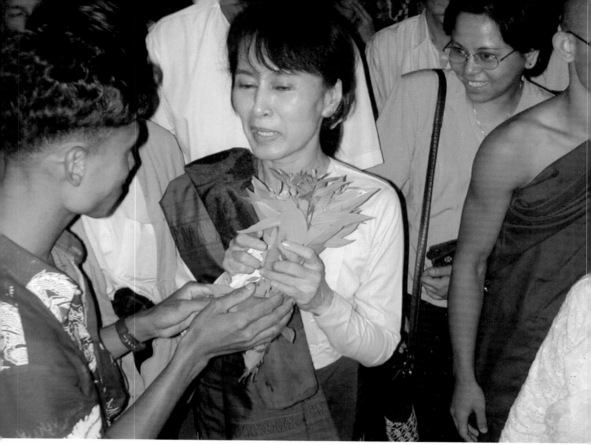

The pro-democracy movement of Aung San Suu Kyi (center) in Myanmar (Burma) is a recent example of nonviolent resistance.

As an editorial in the *Minneapolis Star Tribune* commented, "In the best traditions of Mohandas Gandhi and Martin Luther King, several hundred Nigerian women took a nonviolent stand for their country. Ranging in age from 25 to 90—some with infants strapped to their backs—the women held a successful sit-in at ChevronTexaco's Escravos facility in Nigeria's oil-rich delta. Without firing a shot or injuring a soul, they shut down an operation that produces a half million barrels of oil a day. In the end, they accomplished what their men could not, and what their government should have done long ago.

Over the last one hundred years, this people-power has been witnessed throughout the world. Nonviolent resistance has fueled and guided India's independence, Aung San Suu Kyi's democracy movement in Burma, the movements for change in Eastern and Central Europe that led to the demise of the Soviet Union, the collapse of General Augusto Pinochet's regime in Chile, and the tireless work of the Mothers of the Disappeared that contributed to the end of military dictatorship in Argentina. In late July, 2002, Samdhong Rinpoche, Tibet's prime minister, announced that the Tibetan leadership is in the process of planning a nationwide campaign of Gandhian nonviolent resistance to Chinese rule.

In the United States, virtually every meaningful social transformation has resulted from nonviolent resistance. Women's suffrage, the eight hour work day, ending legalized racial segregation, environmental safeguards, ending the Vietnam War, limiting nuclear testing— these and many other changes were the direct consequence of ordinary citizens clamoring for a better world and translating that longing into embodied moral and political resistance. From the Boston Tea Party to the Underground Railroad to the dramatic nonviolent campaign that led to the passage of the historic American[s with] Disabilities Act, innumerable people have exercised the power of nonviolent resistance to change our society.

Violence Is a Spiritual Crisis

As these historical and contemporary examples suggest, nonviolent resistance is an inward and outward journey of transformation of violent patterns, policies and practices. Violence—any verbal, emotional, physical, institutional or social-structural behavior or condition that dominates, dehumanizes, diminishes or destroys ourselves or others—is a pervasive and daunting reality for the earth and its inhabitants. It is experienced in our inmost being and in the systems and structures that shape the world, including economic exploitation, cultural destruction, racism, sexism, homophobia, militarism and ecological devastation. Rooted in deep inward impulses of fear, hate and greed, these systemic forms of violence and injustice endanger both our survival and our profound hunger for wholeness and integrity.

Nonviolent resistance is a crucially important way to respond to the contemporary pervasiveness of violence. This epidemic represents one of our greatest spiritual crises. But an even deeper crisis may be our pervasive faith in violence, our acknowledged or unacknowledged belief that violence ultimately is just and necessary. "The myth of redemptive violence," as scripture scholar Walter Wink names it, permeates our consciousness and our culture. Hence our age's greatest temptation: to cling to a belief in the effectiveness and preeminence of violence, the conviction that it is "the bottom line," that violence is the final answer. This temptation is rooted in will-to-power or despair, but either attitude repudiates the nonviolent God who longs for our liberation from the scripts, patterns and spiritualities of violence. Nonviolent resistance is a process for challenging violence, but even more deeply it is an embodied practice that helps to free us from our faith in violence—forged in the furnaces of either ambition and self-interest or resignation and capitulation—by opening us to a deeply-grounded faith and trust in the God of compassionate

Most Americans Think Going to War with Iraq Was Wrong

In a nationwide poll conducted November 6–10, 2008, 2,210 registered voters were asked the following question:

Do you think going to war with Iraq was the right thing for the United States to do or the wrong thing?

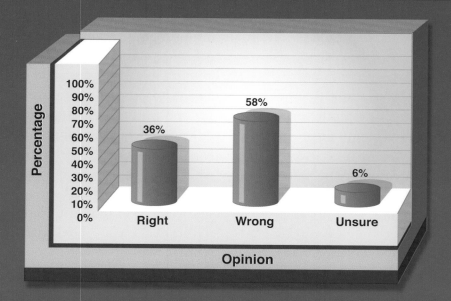

Taken from: Quinnipac University poll, November 6–10, 2008.

nonviolence. Nonviolent resistance is a spiritual practice and a way of being at the service of conversion, the transformation of our selves, our communities and our world.

Jesus Practiced Nonviolence

For two thousand years, Christians have engaged in nonviolent resistance rooted in the vision and practice of Jesus who comprehensively and lovingly resisted violence in its innumerable manifestations. Biblical scholar Nancy Schreck, in her study "The Faithful Nonviolence of Jesus," identifies three foundational dimensions of Jesus' ministry that grounded his nonviolent resistance to violence. First, the inclusive love of God that deems any exclusion as a form of violence. Second, a vision of universal healing. Third, an understanding that God is not a God of vengeance but of radical love who calls us to a spirituality purified of violence at its very roots. Jesus' engaged teaching, practices, and willingness to offer his life were powerful dimensions of his active, creative and deeply nonviolent resistance to all that violates and separates.

Calling this nonviolent resistance may strike some as odd, given that Jesus says in the Gospel of Matthew, "Do not resist an evildoer" (Matt. 5:38–42). But as scripture scholar Walter Wink has documented, the meaning of the original Greek is quite different. While the verb *antistenai* has been almost universally translated as "resist," it is a military term that actually means "resist violently or lethally." Rather than exhorting us to passivity, Jesus urges us to repudiate violence in our response to the evildoer.

This helps make sense of the three teachings which immediately follow this text: the call to turn the other cheek, to give our cloak if someone takes our coat, and to go the extra mile. Instead of enunciating a doctrine of submission, these admonitions exhibit the fundamental dynamic of loving, nonviolent resistance. In a context where his audience would have had firsthand experience with being degraded and treated as an inferior—including being cuffed with the backhand by a master or social superior—to stand one's ground and offer one's left cheek creates in the cultural and political context a dilemma for the perpetrator. As Wink writes, "By turning the cheek, the servant makes it impossible for the master to use the backhand:

his nose is in the way. . . . The left cheek now offers a perfect target for a blow with the right fist; but only equals fought with fists, as we know from Jewish sources, and the last thing the master wishes to do is to establish this underling's equality. This act of defiance renders the master incapable of asserting his dominance in this relationship. . . . By turning the cheek, then, the 'inferior' is saying, 'I'm a human being, just like you. I refuse to be humiliated any longer. I am your equal. I am a child of God. I won't take it anymore.'" Wink reveals how the other saying—about the cloak and going the extra mile—also demonstrate this "third way" between passivity on the one hand and counter-violence on the other.

As Wink suggests, Jesus calls us to practice a nonviolent resistance that is active, not passive; creative, not choreographed. It seizes the moral initiative. It explores a creative alternative to violence. It asserts the dignity and humanity of all parties. It seeks to break the cycle of dehumanization. It faces the consequences of one's action. In proclaiming the love of enemies, it longs to transform "us vs. them" thinking. It works tirelessly for the mutual transformation of the oppressed and the oppressor. By remaining nonviolent—even in the face of severe provocation, intimidation, and threat—such resistance contributes to social transformation in a profound way. In contrast to the coercive and dominative power of violence, nonviolent resistance can unleash the power of truth, love, compassion, justice, and creative collaboration to change lives and whole societies.

Contemporary Christian Nonviolent Resistance

Christians have engaged in nonviolent resistance to injustice and violence since the time of Jesus. In our own era, Dorothy Day, A.J. Muste, André Trocme, Rev. James Lawson, Cesar Chavez, Bishop Leontyne Kelly, Daniel Berrigan, Adolfo Perez Esquivel, Shelley Douglass, Jim Douglass, Bishop Melvin Talbert, Archbishop Desmond Tutu and many others have exemplified the spirituality and practice of Christian nonviolent resistance in their faith-based work for genuine peace and justice. No one in our time has modeled this more clearly than Martin Luther King, Jr. In the midst of the modern Civil Rights movement, Dr. King articulated the vision of the Beloved Community—where no one is excluded—and the role of active, dramatic nonviolence in helping to create this.

Enunciating what he termed "the theology of the sidewalk," King envisioned the process of dismantling structures of injustice as a crucial dimension of the contemporary life of faith. As he wrote, "There is nothing wrong with a traffic law which says you have to stop for a red light. But when a fire is raging, the fire truck goes right through that red light. . . . Or when a [person] is bleeding to death, the ambulance goes through those red lights at top speed. . . . Disinherited people all over the world are bleeding to death from deep social and economic wounds. They need brigades of ambulance drivers who will have to ignore the red lights of the present system until the emergency is solved."

Like King, we face the worldwide emergencies calling for "brigades of ambulance drivers." . . .

> ## Fast Fact
>
> During the entire twentieth century, from 167 to 175 million lives were lost because of wars, and 54 million of these were civilian, according to Zbigniew Brzezinski in *Out of Control: Global Turmoil on the Eve of the Twenty-first Century.*

Call for Nonviolent Action

Now, as the clouds of war gather once again, we as people of faith face another challenging call for nonviolent action. In the wake of the attacks perpetrated on September 11 and the virtually permanent war declared in their wake by President George W. Bush . . . we are called to relentlessly work for true peace and justice. Our history and experience reveal that violence does not breed security. Violence does not end violence. War will not end terrorism. As nonviolence scholar Michael Nagler suggests, water, not fire, quenches fire. We are called to what Walter Wink names the "third way" between passivity on the one hand and counter-violence on the other. To open this space will take courageous and concerted public action.

There are many ways to undertake nonviolent resistance. We can strengthen and deepen groups and circles in local . . . congregations to take action together for alternatives to war and injustice. At Pace e Bene Nonviolence Service, we have developed a process called From

Violence To Wholeness being used by people in a variety of denominations to help ground their work for peace and justice. Whatever process we choose to use, we are called at this critical time to join with one another to pray, reflect, act and support one another in the ways of peace and justice. Together, like the women in Nigeria whose "people-power" helped create a more humane environment, we can take strong and powerful steps toward a world where the well-being of all is translated from vision to reality.

EVALUATING THE AUTHORS' ARGUMENTS:

In this viewpoint Ken Butigan says Christians should always promote nonviolence, while Edward M. McBride asserts in the previous viewpoint that Christians can support "just wars." Using examples from the text, whose argument do you think is more fully supported? Whose argument do you agree with and why?

Viewpoint 5

Violence Cannot Be Resolved with Further Violence

Russell Dickerson

"If you can't fight violence with violence, then perhaps you can unravel it with peace."

In the following viewpoint Russell Dickerson contends that violence does not solve problems. He writes about the movie *Fight Club*, which is based on a novel by Chuck Palahniuk, saying that its premise of using violence to solve a violent problem is senseless. Dickerson argues that peace can solve problems, although with much more difficulty. Dickerson's opinion piece appeared in the *Lumberjack* newspaper, a student-run, independent voice in the city of Flagstaff, Arizona.

AS YOU READ, CONSIDER THE FOLLOWING QUESTIONS:
1. According to Dickerson, what is the problem that the fight club men identify and try to address in the movie?
2. What does Dickerson say is the real-life, present-day parallel to *Fight Club*'s premise?
3. According to Dickerson, politicians are not about to provide a peaceful answer to the violence in Iraq, so the answer will have to come from whom?

Russell Dickerson, "Injecting Violence into Violence Does not Solve Anything," JackCentral, February 22, 2007. www.jackcentral.com. Copyright © 2009 JackCentral. All rights reserved. Reproduced by permission.

Is Violence Necessary? 89

I have a serious problem with *Fight Club*.

Before you start writing a furious e-mail about how culturally unaware I am, I'll acknowledge that it was well written. Chuck Palahniuk is a great author, and he has a keen appreciation for some extremely important social ills our society faces.

The movie has all of the right stylistic touches to make sure it's regarded as hip, edgy and important for a very long time. The acting in it is brilliant, the plot twists are completely unexpected. I really can't say anything bad about it as far as cinema is concerned.

Violence and Injustice Are the Same

My real beef with the film has nothing to do with the aesthetic values by which we judge movies. My problem with *Fight Club* is its premise, which is funny, because the film's premise is really what has won it the most praise. A bunch of men get together and start a club to release male aggression, and they channel their aggression not only into beating each other up but into social rebellion.

Don't get me wrong; I'm all about sticking it to The Man, but think about it. The problem they identify and try to address in the movie is (generally) American capitalism. They're pointing their finger at economic injustice in the movie.

So here's the deal. Injustice and violence are one and the same. Violence is usually understood as physical violence, but really, whether someone's getting punched in the nose or being evicted from an apartment, they're getting hurt, right?

In addition to the victims getting hurt, the perpetrators are being numbed to the dignity of human life—again, this is true whether it's physical violence or another form.

There's a fundamental problem with eschewing violence on one level and embracing it on another. It really doesn't free anyone from the general violence. True, it may substitute one form for another, but it's still violence.

The author says that the movie Fight Club—*which shows young men channeling their aggression by beating each other up—is atually a political statement about injustice.*

This is essentially what Tyler Durden [played by Brad Pitt] advocates in *Fight Club*. He and his followers are infuriated that so many people's lives are so miserable, they attribute it (at least in part) to American capitalism and the credit system, and then they start making dynamite.

Stupid Idea

Does the idea of violently rebelling against a violent system strike anyone else as stupid?

It doesn't seem dumb enough to nearly enough people, by the looks of things though. There's a real-life, present-day parallel, right in front of us.

There's a lot of violence going on in Iraq currently. Some of it is physical, plenty of it is economical, and plenty more is religious and social—and, coincidentally, American capitalism is at the root of a good deal of the violence. And our best idea about how to fix it is to throw a little more violence into the equation.

"Violence solves everything," by Kieran Meehan. www.CartoonStock.com.

At the end of *Fight Club*, Edward Norton's character realizes his movement has spiraled completely out of control, and that violence-driven anarchy isn't quite as romantic as his alter-ego would have him believe.

Things in Iraq are getting tragically closer to violence-driven anarchy by the day. Is there any chance one of the higher-ups in the [George W.] Bush administration will have an epiphany similar to the one *Fight Club*'s narrator (Norton) had any time soon?

Peace

The obvious alternative to violence is peace; if you can't fight violence with violence, then perhaps you can unravel it with peace. The trouble is that it's much, much harder to transform a situation from violent to peaceful than it is to simply inject more violence. Choosing to practice peace is difficult, and it doesn't win elections, which means any issue with violence as the underlying problem isn't going to get much constructive attention.

What we're left with is a violent economic system that's motivating violence in Iraq and neither of them is about to get a peaceful answer from politicians. That'll have to come from us.

> **EVALUATING THE AUTHOR'S ARGUMENTS:**
>
> In this viewpoint Dickerson contends that violence does not solve problems, particularly problems that are violent to begin with, such as those in Iraq. What peaceful methods might be used to solve the problems in Iraq? Do you agree or disagree with Dickerson? Explain.

Chapter 3

How Can Violence Be Prevented?

To prevent violence in American society, many issues, from parental control to gun control, must be addressed.

Parents Should Prevent Youth Violence

Mike Fak

"Rarely it seems, is there any responsibility placed on the parent or parents for allowing their child to learn about life from street thugs and violent movies and music and ill-chosen friends rather than from them."

In the following viewpoint Mike Fak contends that it is parents' responsibility to prevent youth violence. Fak says youth violence prevention is not the responsibility of the schools or even the police. Parents need to stop making excuses for their children, to teach them about life, and to start reprimanding them for bad behavior. Otherwise, says Fak, he sees no end to the numbing violence affecting today's youth. Fak is a writer, columnist, and author of several books.

Mike Fak, "School Violence Demands Responsibility," ProBlogs.com, March 18, 2008. www.problogs.com. Reproduced by permission of the author.

AS YOU READ, CONSIDER THE FOLLOWING QUESTIONS:
1. According to Fak, kids' false sense of image has created what kind of situation?
2. Does Fak think schools and police should provide security at schools?
3. According to the author, how do the Chicago Public School killings differ from those at Columbine High School?

I n Chicago last week [March 2009,] another young man was shot and killed on the streets after school. The 17-year-old African American was shot dead by a 15-year-old African American in what authorities are stating stemmed from a dispute over a hat. A Hat! And that is enough in this day and age to blatantly gun down another human being in front of witnesses thus destroying two lives and two families with just one bullet.

Kids Think Respect Is More Important than Life

The story is new but the topic is not. Too many children believe respect is something so important to them that it supersedes life. This false sense of image has created a situation where every day, students across the country are beaten or wounded or killed all because of some silly notion that the crime is required in order to maintain one's status in a bizarre world of hate and violence. And then the blame is shifted to schools and police and sometimes even the victim.

Rarely it seems, is there any responsibility placed on the parent or parents for allowing their child to learn about life from street thugs and violent movies and music and ill-chosen friends rather than from them.

Often the stories tell of crimes committed in schools in blighted and economically depressed neighborhoods but that is only a trend

FAST FACT

Between July 1999 and June 2006, a total of 116 school-associated homicides occurred among students, according to the U.S. Centers for Disease Control and Prevention.

to the violence and is by no means a requirement. For every ghetto child murdered, there is a tale of another child from a solid middle class family going berserk in a school because he didn't get the respect he believed he deserved. And then we read how it was the failure of the school to provide adequate security or the police for having far too few patrols in an area.

I hate to bring this up but schools and police shouldn't have to provide security at our schools. The initial purpose of schools was to educate, that of police to protect the community against crime. Somewhere along the line, the children attending schools have created a war zone that compels authorities to expend massive amounts of money and time doing something that shouldn't even be occurring in our society. Our schools should be places where our children can

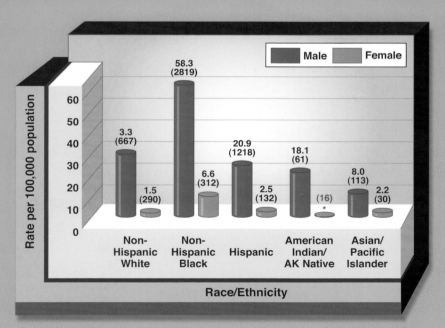

Homicide Rates Among Persons Aged 10–24 Years, by Race/Ethnicity and Sex, United States, 2005

*Race-specific rates and number of deaths (in parentheses) are provided above each bar. Rates are not presented where the number of deaths is fewer than 20 because they are statistically unreliable.

Taken from: U.S. Centers for Disease Control and Prevention, www.cdc.gov/ViolencePrevention/youthviolence/stats_at_a_glance/hr_race-sex_05.html.

The author contends that it is up to parents to prevent youth violence but that, too often, they abdicate responsibility for their childrens' bad actions.

learn and where dreams can start to come true. Our schools should not be a place where dreams are snuffed out and another life is ruined because someone needs to prove to everyone else how much of a "man" they are.

Where Are the Parents?

During all of this the parents take themselves off the hook. They claim their children are good kids and if only the school or police did their job their good kid wouldn't be in jail right now. The blinders, the incredible lack of personal responsibility by parents is enabling this violence to continue to escalate as more and more good sons and daughters prove to the world that no one can disrespect them and live. Never is it the parent's fault that their children walk around the neighborhoods with guns in their pockets and street gang symbols emblazoned on their bodies. Never is it the parent's fault that they don't know what their child is doing and with who. Never when their child starts being arrested does it become apparent that a responsibility to start keeping a watch on their son or daughter and to monitor what they are doing is required of them. Never when they hear the abusive language and talks of violence do they reprimand.

Becoming Numb

In Chicago, the recent murder of [a] 17-year-old [boy] was the eighteenth Chicago Public School killing this year. That is more than the slaughter at Columbine High School. The only difference is these young people were killed one at a time on different days for different silly reasons. It doesn't make these killings any more or less tragic than a mass murder at a school. But like other tragic and troubling news that keeps coming at a steady pace, the stories all start to meld as we become numb to the situation and it all just becomes noise we no longer listen to. And then it happens again to someone we know or love in a neighborhood that until that day we thought was safe.

EVALUATING THE AUTHOR'S ARGUMENTS:

In this viewpoint Mike Fak says that preventing youth violence should be the responsibility of parents. Fak mentions respect in his viewpoint several times. What role does Fak say respect plays in youth violence, and how do you think parents can change this?

Parents Cannot Always Prevent Youth Violence

Dewey G. Cornell

"Parents certainly play an important role in influencing their children, but studies have never found that parents account for the majority of variance in a child's behavior and parent influences are often over-estimated."

In the following viewpoint Dewey G. Cornell asserts that parents' role in preventing violence in their children is limited. Cornell discusses the case of 1997 school shooter Michael Carneal. Cornell contends that Michael's family life was good, he was respectful, and close to his parents. According to Cornell, other factors led Michael to shoot his classmates. These include his developing mental illness, being constantly bullied at school, and the pressure of his peers. Cornell believes poor parenting is not always a factor in youth violence. Cornell is an author, forensic clinical psychologist, and professor in the School of Education at the University of Virginia.

AS YOU READ, CONSIDER THE FOLLOWING QUESTIONS:
1. According to Cornell, as Michael Carneal entered adolescence, his parents recognized that he was struggling with what two things?
2. According to Cornell, the popular kids at Michael Carneal's high school were referred to as what? What were the boys that were not popular referred to as?
3. What were the ages of the students who were killed by Michael Carneal?

There is widespread sentiment that parents play a key role in keeping schools safe. This viewpoint extends to the courtroom, where victims of school shootings have filed lawsuits against parents of the attackers in Pearl, Paducah, Jonesboro, Littleton, and other communities. A cover story in the *New York Times Magazine* pictured the parents of Columbine victim Isaiah Shoels proclaiming, "They ask us if we blame the parents. Who else do we blame?" So far, however, no lawsuit has been successful in finding parents liable for the actions of their child in a school shooting; courts generally rule that parents are not responsible for their children's criminal behavior. The children alone are held responsible, and if they are old enough, they can be tried and punished as adults.

Are bad parents responsible for the school shootings? This is a moral question rather than a scientific one. Parents have legal and moral responsibility for their children, and it is their societal function to raise their children and prepare them for adulthood; thus it makes sense that society would want to hold them accountable when their children commit criminal acts of violence. From a scientific perspective, parents certainly play an important role in influencing their children, but studies have never found that parents account for the majority of variance in a child's behavior and parent influences are often over-estimated.

School shootings are not like other forms of juvenile crime. The typical juvenile offender is raised in a family stressed by problems such as poverty, divorce, domestic violence, parental substance abuse, and

Poll Shows Many Blame Parents for School Shootings

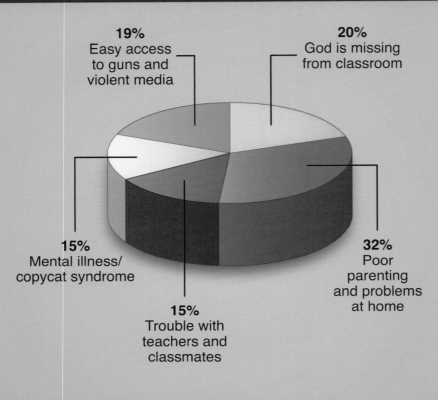

What factor do you think is most responsible for school shootings?

19%
Easy access
to guns and
violent media

20%
God is missing
from classroom

15%
Mental illness/
copycat syndrome

32%
Poor
parenting
and problems
at home

15%
Trouble with
teachers and
classmates

Taken from: Family Education.com poll: The Violence Factor, August 19, 2009.

child abuse and neglect. In contrast the backgrounds of the attackers studied by the Secret Service are quite different. Although some of these students were raised in such adverse circumstances, a surprising number of families appeared to be relatively healthy and well-adjusted.

The Example of Michael Carneal

One example of a seemingly healthy family is that of Michael Carneal, the 14-year-old who killed three students when he fired into a prayer circle at his high school. The 1997 school shooting at Heath High School in West Paducah, Kentucky, has been the subject of considerable study. The police investigation released by the criminal court that sentenced Carneal to life in prison numbered over 2,000 pages in length and the National Research Council commissioned an investigation of school violence that included an extensive case study of the shooting.

The author conducted a forensic evaluation of Michael Carneal for his defense attorneys and testified at his sentencing, during which the court accepted his plea of guilty but mentally ill. The author's forensic evaluation included 20 hours of interviews with Michael, and dozens more with his parents and sister, four grandparents, other relatives, classmates, neighbors, and teachers. The author also had access to records from the police investigation, as well as evaluations conducted by experts for the prosecution and another defense expert. In addition, the author interviewed Michael again seven years later and was able to review the records of his psychiatric treatment in prison.

By all accounts, Mr. and Mrs. Carneal were concerned and dedicated parents. Prior to the school shooting, the Carneals were regarded by friends and relatives as a model family. Mr. Carneal was not only a successful lawyer, but one who was admired by his colleagues for the way he reserved time for his family. Ms. Carneal had a bachelor's degree, but elected to stay at home to raise their two children. The family had meals together, attended church together, and went on regular family trips and vacations. They lived in a well-kept, single-story home in a peaceful, wooded setting. There were no indications of marital conflict, substance abuse, child abuse, or any of the other family problems that one might suspect in a family where a teenager committed a terrible crime.

Michael was close to his mother and father, but somewhat distant with other relatives. He was respectful and obedient at home, and gave his parents little reason to be troubled by misbehavior. As he entered adolescence, they recognized that he was struggling with his self-image and peer relationships, and so tried to be supportive. He was shy and awkward and, at times, unusually fearful. Sometimes he was afraid to go out at night. Occasionally, he refused to sleep in his bedroom and slept on the couch instead. They noticed that whenever he took a shower, he stuffed towels in the bathroom floor vent and made the curious statement that he did not want anyone under the house to see him. Michael's parents did not know quite what to make of their son, but they did not suspect that he was showing signs of mental illness. They also did not know that in previous generations, several relatives had been institutionalized for severe mental illness—including one who had been violent toward others and eventually committed suicide.

If one judged Mr. and Mrs. Carneal by the example of their daughter, it would be impossible to find fault with their parenting. . . .

Bullying

Michael suffered more from teasing and bullying by his peers than from rivalry with his sister [who was popular and successful in school]. In middle school, Michael was a late bloomer: thin and awkward, with oversized glasses and no athletic talent. He became an easy mark for bigger boys who liked to push him around, spit on him, and make fun of him. He was especially troubled when a school gossip column said that he and a male friend "had feelings for one another." A few boys began to call him "gay," "faggot," and other sexually derisive terms.

Michael hoped that things would change when he started high school as a ninth grader, but instead the bullying only worsened. Larger boys continued to call him names and threaten him. They took food from his tray in the cafeteria and dared him to do anything about it. In science class, some of the boys would intentionally ruin his science experiments when the teacher left the room. In another class, several boys liked to put him in a headlock and grind their knuckles into his scalp. Other students experienced similar treatment, but they later reported that Michael seemed more troubled by it, and, as a result, may have been targeted more frequently. . . .

Peer Influences

Michael noticed that many of the boys who teased him were popular with classmates and well regarded by teachers. They were referred to as "preps," a term used by students to refer to a favored or popular group of students. Although Michael and his sister might have been regarded as preps themselves, Michael began to feel alienated from the mainstream at Heath High School. Paranoia, alienation, and acute social anxiety are hallmarks of emerging mental illness.

In contrast to the preps, another group of boys who were not popular were called "freaks," and Michael found himself drawn to them. Why were the freaks appealing? The freaks were also harassed; they supported each another and seemed able to tolerate rejection by their classmates. In fact, they reveled in their marginal status and retaliated by rejecting the social conventions of their peers: they acted independent and defiant and would not participate in the morning prayer group in the school lobby or dress like the preppy students. Some claimed to be Wiccans rather than Christians, although it does not appear that any of them were sincere practitioners of this pagan religion, and used it for shock value.

Most important to Michael, the freaks did not make fun of him and seemed willing to accept him. If Michael could not be accepted by the mainstream group at school, he would turn to the marginal students in this group. It appeared that these older boys—juniors and seniors—took advantage of Michael's eagerness to please them and win their approval: They began to ask him to do small favors and soon he was bringing them gifts like CDs and cash from his father's wallet. . . .

The Shooting

On the day of the shooting, Michael carried two rifles and two shotguns into the school lobby wrapped in a blanket. He set the bundle down by the trophy case where the "freaks" were standing. Some of the boys realized that Michael had guns in the bundle, but none of them accepted his offer to take one. One commented that he "had balls" in bringing the guns to school. Michael also brought a bag of earplugs for the boys, which they also declined. Instead, the boys stood back and watched what happened next.

The prayer group of about 40 students formed a few feet away in the center of the lobby. They joined hands and were led in prayer by one of the students, Ben. Ben was a handsome, muscular senior who played on the football team. His father was pastor of a local church. Ben was also one of the students that Michael had warned specifically not to be in the lobby for the prayer group on Monday. . . .

The bell rang to signal students that it was time to head for their classes. The prayer ended and students dropped hands and bent over to pick up their books and bags. Michael left the bundle of rifles and shotguns alone. Instead, he reached into his book bag and pulled out a .22 caliber Ruger pistol. Fully loaded, the semiautomatic pistol could fire nine shots in rapid succession. . . .

Michael fired eight shots, and each struck a different student. Three girls—ages 14, 15, and 17—were struck in the head and later died in the hospital. A 15-year-old girl was struck in the chest and paralyzed. Two other girls suffered less serious injuries to the shoulder and neck, and two boys suffered minor injuries to the neck and head. It all happened in about 10 seconds.

Still standing in the same spot where he opened fire, Michael put down his gun with one shot remaining. He said that when he saw the blood from the gunshot wounds, he came to his senses and stopped. Immediately after that, Ben came to him from one side, grabbed him by the shoulders and demanded, "What are you doing?" Michael looked at him and replied, "I can't believe I did that—please kill me now.". . .

Lessons for Prevention

Although every case has unique characteristics, the Paducah case provides some important lessons for the prevention of school shootings. First, no single factor can be considered the necessary or sufficient cause of Michael's decision to go on a shooting rampage. Even though parents are obviously the most important influence on a child—and

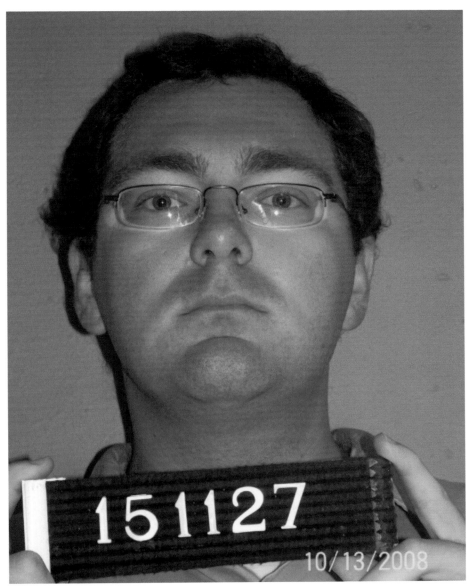

In the case of Michael Carneal, who had a good relationship with his parents, mental illness was a strong factor in his killing of three students at his high school.

the public generally blames parents of students who attack their schools—the Paducah case shows that poor parenting is not always a factor. By all accounts, the Carneals were good parents, and no one would have found fault with them prior to the shooting. One could contend that Michael's parents should have recognized his emerging mental illness, but the symptoms of mental illness are often subtle, and many parents have been stunned to discover that their son or daughter has been quietly delusional or experiencing undetected hallucinations for weeks or even months.

Certainly, Michael's developing mental illness was a critical factor that affected his reasoning and judgment, and made him more vulnerable to other influences. Perhaps Michael's mental illness was the factor that replaced the role often occupied by an abusive or disturbed family. Although most youth who commit serious acts of violence do not have the severity of mental illness that Michael experienced, such cases exist and cannot be ignored.

EVALUATING THE AUTHORS' ARGUMENTS:

In this viewpoint Dewey G. Cornell contends that sometimes mental illness may have more of an impact on school shootings than parents do. However, most people blame the parents for school shootings. Why do you think this is? After reading this viewpoint and the previous viewpoint, what do you think is the most important factor in youth violence?

Gun Control Laws Can Prevent Violence

Garen J. Wintemute

"Americans have purchased millions of guns, predominantly handguns, believing that having a gun at home makes them safer. In fact, handgun purchasers substantially increase their risk of a violent death."

In the following viewpoint Garen J. Wintemute contends that gun violence is an all too common occurrence in the United States, and limiting the availability of guns would prevent this violence. Wintemute says the idea that gun ownership decreases crime is a myth. He says the converse is true. The moment someone buys a gun, they are more likely to die by one. Wintemute also expresses concern about a pending Supreme Court case (it has since been decided) challenging District of Columbia (D.C.) laws that control the use of guns for private citizens. According to Wintemute, if the Supreme Court knocks down the D.C. laws, it could weaken the framework of civil society. The Supreme Court issued its decision in June 2008 and decided to overturn the D.C. gun laws. Wintemute is a professor of emergency medicine and director of the Violence Prevention Research Program at the University of California at Davis School of Medicine, Sacramento.

It is 1992, and schoolmates Yoshihiro Hattori and Webb Haymaker have been invited to a Halloween party. Yoshi, a 16-year-old exchange student and avid dancer, wears a white tuxedo like John Travolta's in *Saturday Night Fever*. By mistake, they stop at a house up the block from their destination. No one answers the doorbell.

Inside are Rodney and Bonnie Peairs. She opens a side door momentarily, sees the boys, and yells to her husband, "Get the gun." He does (it is a .44 magnum Smith & Wesson revolver) and reopens the door. Yoshi and Webb, by now back at the sidewalk, start to return. Yoshi exclaims, "We're here for the party!"

"Freeze!" responds Peairs. Yoshi does not understand the idiom. He approaches the house, repeating his statement about the party. Peairs shoots him once in the chest. Thirty minutes later, Yoshi dies in an ambulance. Bonnie Peairs would later testify, "There was no thinking involved."

Many health care professionals read of such cases without surprise, grimly recognizing in them the familiar picture of gun violence in the United States. That picture also includes the dozens killed and wounded this past year in a terrible series of mass-casualty shootings at educational institutions, shopping malls, places of business, and places of worship, beginning last April 16 at Virginia Tech (33 dead) and ending, for the moment, at a Wendy's restaurant in West Palm Beach, Florida. Many of these innocent people were shot with guns that had been purchased recently and legally.

In 2005, in this country, 30,694 people died from gunshot wounds; 17,002 cases were suicides, 12,352 were homicides, and 1340 were accidental, police-related, or of undetermined intent. Nearly 70,000 more people received treatment for nonfatal wounds in U.S. emergency departments. The disheartening 30% case fatality rate is 18 times that for injuries to motorcyclists. More than 80% of gun-related deaths are pronounced at the scene or in the emergency department; the wounds are simply not survivable. This reality is reflected in the fact that the $2 billion annual costs of medical care for the victims of gun violence are dwarfed by an estimated overall economic burden, including both material and intangible costs, of $100 billion.[1] It's unlikely that health care professionals will soon prevent a greater proportion of shooting victims from dying; rather, we as a society must prevent shootings from occurring in the first place.

Gun violence is often an unintended consequence of gun ownership. Americans have purchased millions of guns, predominantly handguns, believing that having a gun at home makes them safer. In fact, handgun purchasers substantially increase their risk of a violent death. This increase begins the moment the gun is acquired—suicide is the leading cause of death among handgun owners in the first year after purchase—and lasts for years.

> **FAST FACT**
>
> Each day in America 85 people die from guns and another 191 are wounded, according to the Brady Campaign to Prevent Gun Violence.

The risks associated with household exposure to guns apply not only to the people who buy them; epidemiologically, there can be said to be "passive" gun owners who are analogous to passive smokers. Living in a home where there are guns increases the risk of homicide by 40 to 170% and the risk of suicide by 90 to 460%. Young people who commit suicide with a gun usually use a weapon kept at home, and among women in shelters for victims of domestic violence, two thirds of those who come from homes with guns have had those guns used against them.

Legislatures have misguidedly enacted a radical deregulation of gun use in the community. Thirty-five states issue a concealed-weapon permit to anyone who requests one and can legally own guns; two states have dispensed with permits altogether. Since 2005, a total of 14 states have adopted statutes that expand the range of places where people may use guns against others, eliminate any duty to retreat if

Living in a home where guns are kept increases the risk of homicide by 40 to 170 percent and the risk of suicide by 90 to 460 percent.

possible before shooting, and grant shooters immunity from prosecution, sometimes even for injuries to bystanders.

Such policies are founded on myths. One is that increasing gun ownership decreases crime rates—a position that has been discredited.[2] Gun ownership and gun violence rise and fall together. Another myth is that defensive gun use is very common. The most widely quoted estimate, 2.5 million occurrences a year, is too high by a factor of 10.[3]

Policies limiting gun ownership and use have positive effects, whether those limits affect high-risk guns such as assault weapons or Saturday night specials, high-risk persons such as those who have been convicted of violent misdemeanors, or high-risk venues such as gun shows. New York and Chicago, which have long restricted handgun ownership and use, had fewer homicides in 2007 than at any other time since the early 1960s. Conversely, policies that encourage the use of guns have been ineffective in deterring violence. Permissive policies regarding carrying guns have not reduced crime rates, and permissive states generally have higher rates of gun-related deaths than others do.

In 1976, Washington, D.C., took action that was consistent with such evidence. Having previously required that guns be registered, the District prohibited further registration of handguns, outlawed the carrying of concealed guns, and required that guns kept at home be unloaded and either disassembled or locked.

These laws worked. Careful analysis linked them to reductions of 25% in gun homicide and 23% in gun suicide, with no parallel decrease (or compensatory increase) in homicide and suicide by other methods and no similar changes in nearby Maryland or Virginia.[4] Homicides rebounded in the late 1980s with the advent of "crack"

States with More Guns Have More Gun Deaths

States with 5 Highest Gun Death Rates

State	Percentage of Gun Owners	Gun Deaths per 100,000 People
Montana	61.4%	17.22
Arkansas	60.6%	17.49
Alabama	57.2%	16.18
Tennessee	46.4%	16.39
Louisiana	45.6%	19.04

States with 5 Lowest Gun Death Rates

State	Percentage of Gun Owners	Gun Deaths per 100,000 People
New York	18.1%	5.28
Rhode Island	13.3%	3.63
Massachusetts	12.8%	3.48
New Jersey	11.3%	4.99
Hawaii	9.7%	2.20

Taken from: Violence Policy Center, "Pro-Gun States Lead the Nation in per Capita Firearm Death Rates," www.vpc.org/press/0804gundeath.htm, August 20, 2009.

cocaine, but today the District's gun-suicide rate is lower than that of any state.

In 2003, six District residents filed a federal lawsuit alleging that the statutes violated the Second Amendment of the Constitution, which reads, "A well regulated Militia, being necessary to the security of a free State, the right of the people to keep and bear Arms, shall not be infringed." The case was dismissed, but in March 2007, a divided panel of the D.C. Circuit Court of Appeals reversed the dismissal, finding "that the Second Amendment protects an individual right to keep and bear arms," subject to "permissible form[s] of regulatory limitation," as are the freedoms of speech and of the press.[5] The District appealed, and on March 18, 2008, the Supreme Court heard oral arguments in the case of *District of Columbia v. Heller.*

The Court is considering whether the statutes "violate the Second Amendment rights of individuals who are not affiliated with any state-regulated militia, but who wish to keep handguns and other guns for private use in their homes." It will first need to decide whether such rights exist. The District argues, on the basis of the history of the Bill of Rights and judicial precedent, that the Amendment guarantees a right to bear arms only in the service of a well-regulated state militia (which was once considered a vital counterweight to a standing federal army). It argues secondarily that should the Court extend Second Amendment rights to include the possession of guns for private purposes, the statutes remain valid as reasonable limitations of those rights.

No one predicts that a constitutionally protected right to use guns for private purposes, once it's been determined to exist, will remain confined to guns kept at home. Pro-gun organizations have worked effectively at the state level to expand the right to use guns in public, and all but three states generally prohibit local regulation. If people have broadly applicable gun rights under the Constitution, all laws limiting those rights—and criminal convictions based on those laws—will be subject to judicial review. Policymakers will avoid setting other limitations, knowing that court challenges will follow.

Consider Yoshi Hattori's death in light of *District of Columbia v. Heller.* Rodney Peairs was tried for manslaughter. His lawyer summarized Peairs's defense as follows: "You have the legal right to answer everybody that comes to your door with a gun." A Louisiana jury acquitted him after 3 hours' deliberation. That state's laws now justify homicide under many circumstances, including compelling an intruder to leave a dwelling or place of business, and provide immunity from civil lawsuits in such cases. Thirteen other states have followed suit.

A Supreme Court decision broadening gun rights and overturning the D.C. statutes would be widely viewed as upholding such policies. By promoting our sense of entitlement to gun use against one another, it could weaken the framework of ordered liberty that makes civil society possible.

Notes

1. Cook PJ, Ludwig JL. Gun Violence: The Real Costs. Oxford, England: Oxford University Press, 2000.
2. Wellford CF, Pepper JV, Petrie CV, eds. Firearms and Violence: A Critical Review. Washington, DC: National Academies Press, 2004.
3. Hemenway D. Survey Research and Self-Defense Gun Use: An Explanation of Extreme Overestimates. J Crim Law Criminol 1997;87:1430-1445.
4. Loftin C, McDowall D, Wiersema B, Cottey TJ. Effects of Restrictive Licensing of Handguns on Homicide and Suicide In the District of Columbia. N Engl J Med 1991;325:1615-1620.
5. Parker v. District of Columbia, 478 F.3d 370 (D.C. Cir. 2007).

EVALUATING THE AUTHOR'S ARGUMENTS:

In this viewpoint Garen J. Wintemute asserts that gun control laws can prevent violence. What is the primary evidence Wintemute uses to support his argument? Do you think Wintemute is right, that broadening gun rights will lead to a breakdown of civil society? Why or why not?

Viewpoint

4

Gun Control Laws Do Not Prevent Violence

Ted Nugent

"The self-evident truth is that more guns clearly equals less crime."

In the following viewpoint Ted Nugent argues that more gun ownership means less violence. People need guns for self-defense, says Nugent. He asserts that in areas where gun ownership is high, crime is reduced, and in areas with low gun ownership, crime is rampant. Nugent believes it is his and every American's right to own a gun, and that this right should not be taken away because of the "lunatic fringe." Nugent is an American rocker—often called the Motor City Madman—author, avid hunter, and gun rights proponent.

AS YOU READ, CONSIDER THE FOLLOWING QUESTIONS:

1. Nugent says he needs his water, cars, trucks, chainsaws . . . and guns because they are all wonderful ingredients for his American Dream of what?
2. According to Nugent, approximately how many Americans own guns?
3. What does Nugent say about calling 911?

Ted Nugent, "More Guns, Less Violent Crime as the Bad Guys Run or Die," *U.S. News & World Report,* April 20, 2009. Copyright © 2009 U.S. News & World Report, L.P. All rights reserved. Reprinted with permission.

Water, water, everywhere water. Know it, embrace it, manage it, or drown. Same goes for cars, trucks, chainsaws, knives, crowbars, blowtorches, and guns. Based on the inept, clumsy, irresponsible failure of brain-dead, uncoordinated numbnuts, I will not be denied the pragmatic, functional utility of anything.

I will not drown, nor will I drink and drive, chainsaw-massacre anyone, stumble, slice, burn, or shoot myself, nor will I ever hold up a bank. So the best advice would be to think, improvise, adapt, and overcome, man up, but by all means, leave me the hell alone. You don't ban electric guitars just because someone may have a lapse in logic, goodwill, and decency and spontaneously break out into country and western music. The vast majority of sensible people will use electric guitars as God intended and whip out good, sexy rock-n-roll licks.

I need my water, cars, trucks, chainsaws, knives, crowbars, blowtorches, and guns. I have mastered them all; they are all wonderful ingredients for my American Dream of rugged individualism, declared independence, and self-sufficiency. They all serve me well, and I am not giving any of them up. Ever.

Author Ted Nugent (pictured), a gun advocate, contends that where gun ownership is high, crime is reduced and that in areas of low gun ownership, crime is higher.

The masses must never be controlled for the sake of the lunatic fringe. Remember "Don't Tread on Me"? Don't.

America has spoken. With guns and ammo sales and concealed weapons permits surging at unprecedented rates, never in the history of mankind have more people possessed more firepower and most significantly, carried more concealed weapons on their persons than today across America. And as FBI crime reports and law enforcement and academic studies conclude, the self-evident truth is that more guns clearly equals less crime. Where there are more guns per capita, violent crime goes down, particularly crimes of assault, like rape, burglary, and robbery. This is good.

FAST FACT

Americans use guns for self-defense as often as 2.5 million times a year, according to the National Rifle Association.

It is indeed Ted Kennedy's gun ban dream of GunFreeZones that have proven to be the guaranteed slaughter zones where the most innocent lives are lost. Think Columbine, VA Tech, Lane Bryant, NW IL University, Luby's Cafeteria, NJ, Salt Lake City, and Omaha malls, Calgary University, Toronto, Chicago, Boston, Flight 93, the mayor's office in San Francisco, ad nauseam. Peace and love will get you killed, and unarmed helplessness is bad. Unless of course your anthem goes baaa..... baaa...... baaa.

So why in God's good name would any human being wish to force unarmed helplessness on another? That level of cruel indecency and forced victimization is incomprehensible to me and about 100,000,000 Americans who own guns. Self-defense is the most powerful, driving instinct of good people everywhere. To deny this is evil personified. Write this down—GunFreeZones are a felon's playgrounds. Ban GunFreeZones now.

Good people don't want the rapist to succeed. We want him dead. We don't want our homes invaded. We want invaders dead. We don't like carjackers. We like them dead. We don't like armed robbers. We like them dead.

We have examined all the evidence we need to know that calling 911 is a joke, unless of course they bring a dustpan and a mop to clean up the dead monster we just shot while protecting our family.

The choice is clear: Gun control as forced by the Chuck Schumers of the world is complicit in every violent crime committed. Conversely, gun control a la Ted Nugent is putting the second shot through the same hole as the first shot, where innocent lives are saved and recidivistic maggots come to a screeching halt, felled by the lovely ballet of good over evil we call the Double Tap Center

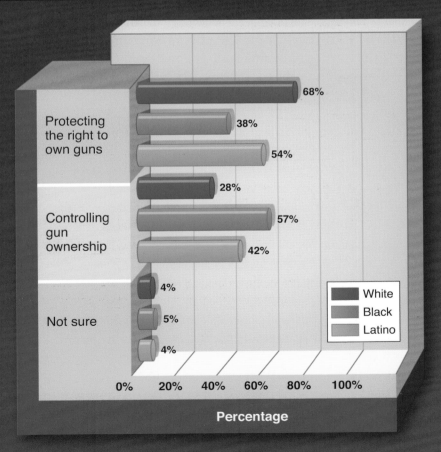

Racial Differences in Gun Ownership Views

What do you think is more important — protecting the right of Americans to own guns or controlling gun ownership?

Protecting the right to own guns
- White: 68%
- Black: 38%
- Latino: 54%

Controlling gun ownership
- White: 28%
- Black: 57%
- Latino: 42%

Not sure
- White: 4%
- Black: 5%
- Latino: 4%

0%   20%   40%   60%   80%   100%

Percentage

Legend:
- White
- Black
- Latino

Taken from: YouGovPollingPoint, "Pro-Gun States Lead the Nation in per Capita Firearm Death Rates," www.pollingpoint.com/result/7, August 20, 2009.

Mass Boogie. Learn it, know it, love it, shoot it. Good guys should live, bad guys not so much.

It is reassuring, and ultimately convenient, that fresh from escaping the scourges of tyranny, slavery, kings, and emperors, our brilliant, sensible Founding Fathers knew it was important to write down the self-evident truth that the right to self-defense is surely a God-given individual right to keep and bear arms. Write this down, too—"keep" means it is mine, you can't have it. "Bear" means I've got them right here on me. "Shall not be infringed" echoes that beautiful "Don't Tread On Me" chorus.

I like the U.S. Constitution and our sacred Bill of Rights but, quite frankly, I don't really need them in order to know in my heart and soul the list of self-evident truths therein. Those came from thinking, common-sense men who refused to be helpless, dependent slaves to anyone or anything. These truths are all burned forever on my soul. I live them, no matter what.

Meanwhile, in order to stop the drowning and murders, I will work on banning water; Obama can try to ban guns. Good luck.

EVALUATING THE AUTHORS' ARGUMENTS:

In this viewpoint Ted Nugent contends that gun ownership is an American right and that it reduces crime. Compare the style and tone of Nugent's viewpoint with the style and tone of the previous viewpoint by Garen J. Wintemute. Which viewpoint do you think is more effective and why?

Facts About Violence

Editor's note: These facts can be used in reports or papers to reinforce or add credibility when making important points or claims.

Facts About Youth Violence

According to the U.S. Centers for Disease Control and Prevention:

- In 2006, 5,958 young people aged ten to twenty-four were murdered—an average of sixteen each day.
- Homicide was the second leading cause of death for young people aged ten to twenty-four.
- Among ten- to twenty-four-year-olds, homicide is the leading cause of death for African Americans, the second-leading cause of death for Hispanics, and the third-leading cause of death for Asian/Pacific Islanders and American Indians and Alaska Natives.
- Among ten- to twenty-four-year-olds, 87 percent (5,159) of homicide victims were male and 13 percent (799) were female.
- Among homicide victims aged ten to twenty-four, 84 percent were killed with a firearm.
- In 2007 more than 668,000 young people aged ten- to twenty-four were treated in emergency departments for injuries sustained from violence.
- In a 2007 nationally representative sample of youth in grades nine through twelve, 35.5 percent reported being in a physical fight in the twelve months preceding the survey and 18.0 percent reported carrying a weapon (gun, knife, or club) on one or more days in the thirty days preceding the survey.

Facts About School Violence

According to the 2008 edition of *Indicators of School Crime and Safety* issued by the U.S. Bureau of Justice Statistics and the National Center for Education Statistics:

- Among youth aged five to eighteen, thirty-five school-associated violent deaths (twenty-seven homicides and eight suicides) occurred from July 1, 2006, through June 30, 2007.

- Among students aged twelve to eighteen, about 767,000 were victims of violent crimes in 2006.
- During the 2005–2006 school year, 86 percent of public schools reported that at least one violent crime, theft, or other crime occurred at their school.
- In 2007, 8 percent of students in grades nine through twelve reported being threatened or injured with a weapon in the previous twelve months.
- In 2007, 2 percent of students aged twelve to eighteen reported being the victim of a serious violent crime at school during the previous six months.
- In 2007, 10 percent of students aged twelve to eighteen reported that someone at school had used hate-related words against them.
- In 2007, 23 percent of students aged twelve to eighteen reported that gangs were at their schools.
- In 2007, 32 percent of students aged twelve to eighteen reported having been bullied at school during the school year.
- In 2005–2006, 24 percent of public schools reported that student bullying was a daily or weekly problem.
- In 2007, 12 percent of students in grades nine through twelve reported they had been in a fight on school property during the preceding twelve months.
- In 2007, 6 percent of students in grades nine through twelve reported they had carried a weapon on school property during the previous thirty days.
- In 2007, approximately 5 percent of students aged twelve to eighteen reported that they were afraid of attack or harm at school.

Facts About Domestic Violence

According to the Family Violence Prevention Fund:

- On average more than three women a day are murdered by their husbands or boyfriends in the United States.
- In 2005, 1,181 women were murdered by an intimate partner.
- In 2008 the Centers for Disease Control and Prevention published data collected in 2005 that finds that women experience 2 million injuries from intimate partner violence each year.
- Nearly one in four women in the United States reports experiencing violence by a current or former spouse or boyfriend at some point in her life.

- There were 248,300 rapes/sexual assaults in the United States in 2007, more than 500 per day, up from 190,600 in 2005.
- The U.S. Justice Department's Bureau of Justice Statistics estimates that 3.4 million persons said they were victims of stalking during a twelve-month period in 2005 and 2006; twenty stalking victimizations per one thousand females aged eighteen and older, and approximately seven stalking victimizations per one thousand males aged eighteen and older.
- Young women aged twenty to twenty-four experience the highest rates of rape and sexual assault, followed by those sixteen to nineteen.
- Approximately one in three adolescent girls in the United States is a victim of physical, emotional, or verbal abuse from a dating partner.
- Teen victims of physical dating violence are more likely than their nonabused peers to smoke, use drugs, engage in unhealthy diet behaviors (taking diet pills or laxatives and vomiting to lose weight), engage in risky sexual behaviors, and attempt or consider suicide.
- About 15.5 million children in the United States live in families in which partner violence occurred at least once in the past year, and 7 million children live in families in which severe partner violence occurred.
- In a single day in 2008, 16,458 children were living in a domestic violence shelter or transitional housing facility. Another 6,430 children sought services at a nonresidential program.
- Women who have experienced domestic violence are 80 percent more likely to have a stroke, 70 percent more likely to have heart disease, 60 percent more likely to have asthma, and 70 percent more likely to drink heavily than women who have not experienced intimate partner violence.
- The United Nations Development Fund for Women estimates that at least one of every three women globally will be beaten, raped, or otherwise abused during her lifetime. In most cases, the abuser is a member of her own family.

Facts About Violent Deaths Around the World
According to the World Health Organization:
- Each year, over 1.6 million people worldwide lose their lives to violence.

- In 2000, an estimated 520,000 homicides occurred, or 8.8 per 100,000 population.
- Male victims accounted for 77 percent of all homicides and had rates that were more than three times those of female victims (13.6 and 4.0, respectively, per 100,000).
- The highest rates of homicide in the world are found among males aged fifteen to twenty-nine years (19.4 per 100,000), followed closely by males aged thirty to forty-four years (18.7 per 100,000).
- Worldwide, suicide claimed the lives of an estimated 815,000 people in 2000, or 14.5 per 100,000.
- Over 60 percent of all suicides occurred among males, over half of these occurring among those aged fifteen to forty-four years.
- In 2000 the rate of violent death in low- to middle-income countries was 32.1 per 100,000 population, more than twice the rate in high-income countries (14.4 per 100,000).
- In the African Region and the Region of the Americas, homicide rates are nearly three times greater than suicide rates.
- In the European and South-East Asia Regions, suicide rates are more than double homicide rates.
- In the Western Pacific Region, suicide rates are nearly six times greater than homicide rates.

Facts About Guns

- According to the National Rifle Association, more than 250 million firearms are privately owned in the United States, and the number of new guns increases by about 4.5 million each year.
- Currently, forty-eight out of the fifty United States allow some type of concealed weapon permit which allows a person to carry a concealed weapon.
- According to the National Crime Victimization Survey in 2005, 477,040 victims of violent crimes stated that they faced an offender with a firearm.
- Incidents involving a firearm represented 9 percent of the 4.7 million violent crimes of rape and sexual assault, robbery, and aggravated and simple assault in 2005, according to the National Crime Victimization Survey.
- The FBI's *Crime in the United States* estimated that 66 percent of the 16,137 murders in 2004 were committed with firearms.

Organizations to Contact

The editors have compiled the following list of organizations concerned with the issues debated in this book. The descriptions are derived from materials provided by the organizations. All have publications or information available for interested readers. The list was compiled on the date of publication of the present volume; the information provided here may change. Be aware that many organizations take several weeks or longer to respond to inquiries, so allow as much time as possible for the receipt of requested materials.

Beyond War
302 E. Hersey, Ste. 7
Ashland, OR 97520
(541) 488-5525
fax: (541) 488-5525
e-mail: beyondwar@beyondwar.org
Web site: www.beyondwar.org

Beyond War is a community of people around the world committed to ending the use of warfare in this century. The organization explores, models, and promotes practical ways of resolving conflict. Beyond War understands that conflict is inevitable, but war is not. They base their work on three guiding principles: War is obsolete, we are one on this planet, and the means are the ends in the making. The organization works through several initiatives to increase public awareness and educate people about the possibility of a world without war. The Web site offers educational tools such as the video *Building a World Beyond War: A Roadmap for Citizens.*

Brady Center to Prevent Gun Violence
1225 Eye St. NW, Ste. 1100
Washington, DC 20005
(202) 289-7319

fax: (202) 408-1851

Web site: http://bradycenter.org

The Brady Center to Prevent Gun Violence and its legislative and grassroots affiliate, the Brady Campaign to Prevent Gun Violence, is the nation's largest nonpartisan grassroots organization leading the fight to prevent gun violence. The organization was formed by Sarah and Jim Brady. Jim Brady, the former press secretary for Ronald Reagan, was shot in 1982 during an assassination attempt on the president. The organization works to enact and enforce sensible gun laws, regulations, and policies; to educate children and adults about gun violence; and to reform the gun industry. The organization's *Brady Report Online* and Web site provide up-to-date news about guns in America.

Family Violence Prevention Fund (FVPF)

383 Rhode Island St., Ste. 304

San Francisco CA 94103

(415) 252-8900

fax: (415) 252-8991

e-mail: info@endabuse.org

Web site: www.endabuse.org

The FVPF believes everyone has a right to a life without violence. The organization works to end violence against women and children around the world and to help those who have been victims of violence. FVPF promotes violence prevention efforts and educates health care providers, police, judges, employers, and others about ways to address violence. The organization's Web site offers many materials about children and domestic violence.

Military Operations Research Society (MORS)

1703 N. Beauregard St., Ste. 450

Alexandria, VA 22311

(703) 933-9070

fax: (703) 933-9066

MORS comprises defense analysts, operators, and managers from government, industry, and academia. The objective of MORS is to enhance the quality and effectiveness of operations research as applied to national security issues. MORS publications include the *Military Operations Research Society Journal* and *Phalanx*.

National Center for Children Exposed to Violence (NCCEV)
Yale University, Child Study Center
230 S. Frontage Rd.
New Haven, CT 06520
(877) 496-2238
fax: (203) 785-4608

The mission of the NCCEV is to increase the capacity of individuals and communities to reduce the incidence and impact of violence on children and families; to train and support the professionals who provide intervention and treatment to children and families affected by violence; and, to increase professional and public awareness of the effects of violence on children, families, communities, and society. The NCCEV Resource Center provides public access to a wide variety of materials on children's exposure to violence within homes, schools, and communities.

National Center for Victims of Crime (NCVC)
2000 M St. NW, Ste. 480, Washington, DC 20036
(202) 467-8700
fax: (202) 467-8701
e-mail: webmaster@ncvc.org
Web site: www.ncvc.org

The NCVC is the nation's leading resource and advocacy organization for crime victims and those who serve them. The NCVC works with grassroots organizations and criminal justice agencies throughout the United States to serve millions of crime victims. The center provides direct services and resources to crime victims; advocates for laws and public policies that secure rights, resources, and protections for crime victims; delivers training and technical assistance to victim service organizations, counselors, attorneys, criminal justice agencies, and allied professionals serving victims of crime; and fosters cutting-edge thinking about the impact of crime and the ways in which each person can help victims of crime rebuild their lives. The NCVC Web site provides many of the organization's reports and studies, such as *Snitches Get Stitches*, *Teen Action Toolkit*, and *Our Vulnerable Teenagers*.

National Rifle Association (NRA)
11250 Waples Mill Rd.
Fairfax, VA 22030

(800) 672-3888
Web site: www.nra.org

The NRA is a nationwide organization whose mission is to preserve and defend the U.S. Constitution, especially the inalienable right to keep and bear arms guaranteed by the Second Amendment. The NRA has many publications, including *American Rifleman*, *American Hunter*, and *America's 1st Freedom.*

National Youth Rights Association (NYRA)
1101 Fifteenth St., NW Ste. 200
Washington, DC 20005
(202) 296-2992 x131
Web site: www.youthrights.org
Facebook: www.facebook.com/YouthRights

The NYRA is a national youth-led organization whose mission is to advocate for the legal and civil rights of young people in the United States. NYRA educates people about youth rights, empowers young people to work on their own behalf, and takes direct steps to lessen the burden of ageism. NYRA members work to lower the voting age, lower the drinking age, repeal curfews, protect student rights, and fight age discrimination.

Pace e Bene
2501 Harrison St.
Oakland, CA 94612
(510) 268-8765
fax: (510) 268-8799
e-mail: info@paceebene.org
Web site: www.paceebene.org

Pace e Bene is a nonprofit international organization composed of people from a diversity of spiritual traditions and cultural backgrounds. Pace e Bene envisions dignity, justice, and peace for all. The organization's mission is to foster a just and peaceful world through education about nonviolence, community-building, and action. The organization collaborates with international, national, and local organizations, religious communities, and movements taking nonviolent action to foster just and lasting peace, champion human rights, challenge the violence of poverty and multiple forms of oppression, and strengthen spiritually-based initiatives for justice and peace. Pace e Bene publishes books such as *Exploring Nonviolent Living, From Violence to Wholeness,* and *Traveling with the Turtle: Women's Spirituality of Peacemaking.* Pace e Bene's quarterly newsletter is called the *Wolf.*

Society for Military History
c/o Kurt Hackemer
Dept. of History, University of South Dakota
414 E. Clark St.
Vermillion, SD 57069
(605) 677-5571
e-mail: kurt.hackemer@usd.edu
Web site: www.smh-hq.org

The Society for Military History is devoted to stimulating and advancing the study of military history. The organization holds annual meetings, each of which focuses on an examination of military institutions and practices. For instance, the 2010 annual meeting focused on the causes, conduct, resolution, and consequences of past wars. The society publishes the *Journal of Military History* and issues the quarterly newsletter *Headquarters Gazette.*

Tanenbaum
254 W. Thirty-first St., 7th Fl.
New York, NY 10001
(212) 967-7707
fax: (212) 967-9001
Web site: www.tanenbaum.org

Tanenbaum is a secular, nonsectarian organization that believes that the abuse of religion threatens world peace. The organization works to reduce and prevent violence perpetrated in the name of religion by supporting religious peacemakers who struggle in areas of armed conflict and by overcoming religious intolerance in workplaces and schools. Tanenbaum helps teachers to prepare students to live in a multicultural, multireligious society; works with corporations and institutions to create religiously inclusive policies and practices; trains service providers in health care and other settings to work with religiously diverse communities; and identifies, trains, and promotes religious peacemakers from far and near—so they are even more effective in areas of armed conflict. Tanenbaum publishes many books promoting interreligious understanding, such as the *Interreligious Understanding Guidebook* and the *Medical Manual for Religio-Cultural Competence: Caring for Religiously Diverse Populations.* The organization issues a periodic newsletter, the *Tanenbaum Report,* and publishes each year's Tanenbaum Memorial Lecture, such as Madame Jehan Sadat's 1996 Memorial Lecture *Religion & World Peace: A Muslim's View.*

Violence Policy Center (VPC)
1730 Rhode Island Ave. NW, Ste. 1014
Washington, DC 20036
(202) 822-8200
e-mail: www.vpc.org/contact.htm
Web site: www.vpc.org

The VPC is a nonprofit organization based in Washington, D.C., that works to prevent gun violence. The VPC approaches gun violence as a public health issue, advocating that firearms be subject to health and safety standards like those that apply to virtually all other consumer products. The VPC works through research, advocacy, and education. Each year the VPC publishes various reports such as *American Roulette: Murder-Suicide in the United States, Iron River: Gun Violence and Illegal Firearms Trafficking on the U.S.-Mexico Border,* and *Youth Gang Violence and Guns: Data Collection in California.*

For Further Reading

Books

Ames, Mark. *Going Postal: Rage, Murder, and Rebellion: From Reagan's Workplaces to Clinton's Columbine and Beyond.* New York: Soft Skull, 2005. Takes a systematic look at the scores of rage killings in public schools and the workplace that have occurred since the 1980s. Argues that such killings are acts of political insurgency rather than ordinary crimes or the actions of disturbed individuals.

Burns, Charlene. *More Moral than God: Taking Responsibility for Religious Violence.* Lanham, MD: Rowman & Littlefield, 2008. Draws from psychology, philosophy, and theology to examine the motivations behind religious violence. Provides a brief history of religious violence and addresses other possible motivations, including politics, economics, globalization, family dynamics, and more.

Cornell, Dewey. *School Violence: Fears Versus Facts.* New York: Routledge, 2006. A forensic psychologist uses case studies to identify myths and misconceptions about youth violence, from bullying to rampage shootings.

Kelly, Caitlin. *Blown Away: Women and Guns.* New York: Pocket Books, 2004. Chronicles the history of gun-owning American women and examines the impact guns have on women and society at large. Presents revealing conversations with a diverse group of women, including gun owners, gun control activists, those who have survived violent assaults, and those who have used guns for self-defense.

Kutner, Lawrence, and Cheryl Olson. *Grand Theft Childhood.* New York: Simon & Schuster, 2008. Founders of the Harvard Medical School Center for Mental Health and Media examine whether video games are responsible for a rise in social violence. Provides even-handed information on violence and video games.

Lott, John, Jr. *More Guns, Less Crime: Understanding Crime and Gun Control Laws.* Chicago: University of Chicago Press, 2000. Contends that crime rates go down as more people own guns.

Discusses responses to a controversial study the author published in 1997 that showed that concealed-carry weapons permits reduced the crime rate.

Moffatt, Gregory. *Stone Cold Souls: History's Most Vicious Killers.* Westport, CT: Greenwood, 2008. Provides a detailed examination of some of the most brutal killers in history. Looks at historical accounts of events and analyzes them from a psychological perspective. Discusses different types of killers, presents case studies and historical contexts, and describes what sets these cases apart from other kinds of killings.

Myers, Winslow. *Living Beyond War: A Citizen's Guide.* Maryknoll, NY: Orbis, 2009. Explores practical ways to resolve conflicts without violence and to address human needs directly.

Webber, Julie. *Failure to Hold: The Politics of School Violence.* Lanham, MD: Rowman & Littlefield, 2003. Examines school violence in the United States in the late 1990s in an attempt to locate the blind spots of democratic political culture.

Periodicals and Internet Sources

Abuzeid, Huda. "Why Has My Father's Murder Gone Unpunished?" *Spectator*, August 26, 2009.

America's Intelligence Wire. "Experts: Loss, Revenge Often Drive Mass Murders," August 10, 2009.

Brasier, L.L., John Wisely, and Joe Swickard, "36 Youths Charged with Murders for Lunch Money, Texts, Thrills." *Detroit Free Press*, September 3, 2009.

Codrea, David. "Rights Watch: A Red Herring," *Guns Magazine*, August 2009.

Connecticut Law Tribune. "When Domestic Violence Comes to Work," July 27, 2009.

Economist. "The New Wars of Religion," November 1, 2007.

———. "Taking on the Unholy Family: Mexico's Drug Gangs," July 25, 2009.

Erb, Robin. "Crime on Campus a Harsh Teacher," *Detroit Free Press*, August 23, 2009.

Forelle, Charles. "The Snap Judgment on Crime and Unemployment," *Wall Street Journal*, April 15, 2009.

Jonsson, Patrik. "Shootings, Murder-Suicide Raise Broader Question: Is Violence Linked to Recession?" *Christian Science Monitor*, March 30, 2009.

Kierkegaard, Patrick. "Video Games and Aggression," *International Journal of Liability and Scientific Enquiry*, May 14, 2008.

Küng, Hans. "Religion, Violence and 'Holy Wars,'" *International Review of the Red Cross*, June 2005.

Maxwell, Lynne. "Why We Kill," *Library Journal*, April 1, 2005.

Ritter, Nancy. "Missing Persons and Unidentified Remains: The Nation's Silent Mass Disaster," *National Institute of Justice Journal*, January 2007.

Simons, Lewis. "Genocide and the Science of Proof," *National Geographic*, January 2006.

Slovic, Paul. "If I Look at the Mass I Will Never Act: Psychic Numbing and Genocide," *Judgment and Decision Making*, April 2007.

Virginia Tech Review Panel. *Mass Shootings at Virginia Tech*, April 16, 2007. www.vtreviewpanel.org. The Virginia Tech shootings are reviewed by a panel of experts. Discusses the handling of the incident by police, emergency responders, and the university. Reviews services provided to survivors and victims' families after the shootings. Findings include ways to prevent such tragedies and to assist police and others with appropriate responses to such incidents.

Whittington-Egan, Richard. "The Serial Killer Phenomenon," *Contemporary Review*, Autumn 2008.

Women's Health Weekly. "Pittsburgh Fitness Center Attack Only Most Recent Mass Shooting Committed by Concealed Handgun Permit Holder," August 20, 2009.

Zerwick, Phoebe. "Why Didn't They Stop Him?" *Oprah Magazine*, August 2009.

Web Sites

Bureau of Justice Statistics (www.ojp.usdoj.gov/bjs/welcome.html). The Bureau of Justice Statistics (BJS) is a division of the U.S. Department of Justice, the top law enforcement agency in the country. The BJS serves as the United States' primary source for criminal justice statistics. The BJS Web site provides data on crime, criminal offenders, victims of crime, and the operation of justice systems at all levels of government.

National Coalition Against Domestic Violence (www.ncadv.org). The National Coalition Against Domestic Violence (NCADV) is "a grassroots non-profit organization founded in 1978 to end violence in the lives of women and children." The NCADV's Web site provides information on all of the organization's programs, activities, and events as well as information on legislative issues, domestic violence research material, and other related topics.

National Youth Violence Prevention Resource Center (www .safeyouth.org). The National Youth Violence Prevention Resource Center (NYVPRC) was established in 1999 by the U.S. Centers for Disease Control and Prevention and the White House Council on Youth Violence. The NYVPRC Web site serves as a source of information about youth violence and provides resources to help local communities prevent youth violence.

U.S. Centers for Disease Control and Prevention Violence Prevention Website (www.cdc.gov/violenceprevention/index .html). The U.S. Centers for Disease Control and Prevention (CDC) considers violence a serious public health issue. The agency's violence prevention Web site provides information on youth violence, suicide, sexual violence, school violence, and many other types of violence.

Index

A

The Ambivalence of the Sacred (Appleby), 24

Amen, Daniel, 37–38

American Psychological Association (APA), 9

American Sociological Review (journal), 30

American Violence (Hofstadter), 42–43

Anderson, Craig, 46

Appleby, R. Scott, 24

Ashcroft, John, 22

Atlantic (magazine), 24

Augustine (saint), 71, 72, 76

Aung San Suu Kyi, 82, *82*

B

Baghdad, Iraq, 19–21

Batek people (Malaysia), 68, *69*

Begley, Sharon, 33

Beirut, Lebanon, 15–16

Belfast, Northern Ireland, 14–15

Belgrade, Serbia, 17–18

Berrigan, Daniel, 86

Bethlehem, 18

bin Laden, Osama, 21

Bombay, India, 16–17

Brady Campaign to Prevent Gun Violence, 11

Brain activity, 37–38, 40

Brumfield, Michael, 8

Brzezinski, Zbigniew, 87

Bullying, 7–10

as factor in school shootings, 104

prevalence of, 105

Bullying.org (Web site), 9

Bureau of Justice Statistics, U.S., 90

Bush, George W., 87, 93

Butigan, Ken, 80

C

Canadian Conference of Bishops, 71, 78

Carneal, Michael, 8, 102–108, *107*

Catechism of the Catholic Church, 74–77

Catholic Church, 25

Catholic just war doctrine, 70–79

Centers for Disease Control and Prevention (CDC), 7, 96

Chavez, Cesar, 86

Child abuse/neglect, 37

Childhood, 39–40

Children

innate temperament and treatment of, 40

value respect over life, 96–98

video game habits and later behavior, 46, 48

Cho Seung-Hui, 34, *35, 43, 55, 62*

Cornell, Dewey G., 100

Crusades, 14, 19

from guns in homes, 111
Sunni Islam, 25
Surveys
    on American's support for
      invasion of Iraq, *84*
    on factors in school shootings,
      102
    on protecting right to own, *119*

T
Talbert, Melvin, 86
Thomas Aquinas (saint), 71, 72
Thompson, Jack, 52
Thucydides, 63–64
Tocqueville, Alexis de, 43
Trocme, André, 86
Tutu, Desmond, 86

U
United States
    homicide rate in other nations
      vs., 43
    nonviolent resistance in, 83
    trends in homicide rate, *63*
U.S. Constitution, 114

V
Video games
    are a cause of violence, 45–50
    do not cause violence, 51–58
    by rating and units sold, *55*
Violence
    cannot be resolved by further
      violence, 89–93
    Christian just war doctrine
      allows, 70–79
    genes alone do not cause, 33–44
    genes play a role in, 28–32
    gun control laws can prevent,
      109–115

gun control laws do not prevent,
    116–120
is a part of human nature,
    60–64
is not necessarily a part of
    human nature, 65–69
religion does not cause, 23–27
religion is a cause of, 12–22
as spiritual crisis, 83–85
video games are a cause of,
    45–50
video games do not cause, 51–58
Virginia Tech shooting, 54
Volf, Miroslav, 23
Vonnegut, Kurt, 62

W
Walker-Hoover, Carl, 7, 8
Walsh, David, 49–50
War(s). *See also* Just war doctrine
    percentage of time spent at, *26*
    20th century, 87
Whitman, Charles, 34
Wilson, Latricia, 8
Wink, Walter, 83, 85, 86
Wintemute, Garen J., 109
Wiretap.org (Web site), 9
World Health Organization
    (WHO), 36

Y
Youth violence
    most violent crimes, by gender,
      30
    parents cannot always prevent,
      100–108
    parents should prevent, 95–99

Z
al-Zarqawi, Abu Musab, 20, 21

Picture Credits